CITIZENS & EXILES
CHRISTIAN FAITHFULNESS IN GOD'S TWO KINGDOMS

SCOTT ANIOL

 Press

Citizens and Exile: Christian Faithfulness in God's Two Kingdoms

Copyright © 2023 by Scott Aniol

Published by G3 Press
4979 GA-5
Douglasville, GA 30135
www.G3Min.org

All rights reserved. No part of this publication may be reproduced, stored in a retrieval system, or transmitted in any form by any means, electronic, mechanical, photocopy, recording, or otherwise, without prior permission of the publisher, except as provided for by USA copyright law.

Scripture quotations are from the ESV® Bible (*The Holy Bible, English Standard Version®*), copyright © 2001 by Crossway, a publishing ministry of Good News Publishers. Used by permission. All rights reserved. All emphases in Scripture quotations have been added by the author.

Printed in the United States of America by Graphic Response, Atlanta, GA.

ISBN: 978-1-959908-13-5

CONTENTS

Foreword i

Introduction 1

1 God's Two Kingdoms 9

2 Dual Citizens 33

3 Remember Who We Are 51

4 Christian Faithfulness 73

5 God's Servants for Our Good 93

6 Culture Makers 117

7 The Church's Mission 135

8 Worship Is Warfare 155

Conclusion 177

Appendix: Review of *Mere Christendom* by Douglas Wilson 183

FOREWORD

The church of the Lord Jesus Christ is called to be "stable and steadfast" (Col 1:23). Steadiness is not high on the list of desirable traits among Christians today, however. In evil days, we are greatly tempted to be anything but steady; from some understandable motives, we seek extreme solutions, radical proposals, and try to ramp the church up to fight fire with fire. As one common example, if we see our country slipping into darkness (as it surely is), then we need to punch back and take it over.

This sounds appealing to many. We can grasp why. It is good for Christians to have great influence in their context, and I am thankful for Christians who have that desire. But here is the problem: without even knowing or intending it, we can end up drifting from the central mission of Christ's church. That mission, as Scott Aniol helpfully articulates, is to make disciples in fulfillment of the Great Commission, teaching them a holistic Christianity centered in the redeeming gospel that affects all of life (Matthew 28:16-20). A vibrant church will have 10,000 salutary effects in a given society, rendering believers nothing less than the "salt and light" of it (Matt 5:16-20).

The faithful church hews close, very close, to the Scripture. We mind our mandate. Today, however,

Christians are urged to embrace proposals for Christian action and influence that—in the frankest terms—are not firmly and incontestably grounded in New Testament exegesis. The aforementioned push to "Christianize" the nation and create a new "Christendom" fits this category. So too, in far more troubling terms, does the exhortation to preserve our distinct ethnicity through ethnically homogeneous marriages and families and churches. Doing so, we hear, is essential to forming a "Christian nation."

While we want a public square strongly influenced by biblical truth, I contend that the above ideals do not represent our new covenant mission. (I say this, by the way, with awareness that there are different streams of "Christian nationalism," some of them more intentionally exegetical and worthy of consideration, others less so.) I need not offer a case for this; Scott Aniol does that in the pages to come. But I can simply affirm what is laid out in this text: we are most essentially citizens of the kingdom of Christ, as Aniol elegantly shows here. We are not trying to form a Christian commonwealth; we are already a "holy nation" through the blood of Christ (1 Pet 2:9). This nation is not a project we are building in our strength by our schemes and our activism; this holy nation is what God is building through the gospel of divine grace.

I believe this is an important conviction to state. Of course, I also hold that Christians can disagree about many particulars. Even where the Bible speaks, we have much freedom to work out what biblical obedience looks like when fleshed out. As one example of this, we can and will differ over precisely how we engage government in a fallen world. There are all sorts of matters that require careful handling, and where we face them, we do well to walk in humility and charity. Yet with this stated, I repeat myself: we simply do not have freedom to tweak, let alone overhaul, the mission of the church.

Thankfully, many are grasping this afresh in our time. Theological camps that once fought with one another are now finding more and more unity. At the level of historical theology, I can say without blushing that I track with Abraham Kuyper. I want a vivified church and a robust public theology. But as I read the material of explicit 2K advocates, I see growing convergence of conviction between "two kingdoms" theology and Kuyperianism. The two systems may not be exactly the same, but advocates of each system (like Aniol and me) find ourselves agreeing a good deal more often than we differ. This is a heartening development.

To put this succinctly, some "2K" aficionados emphasize cultural engagement more than in past days. Some in the Kuyperian crowd emphasize the spiritual mission of the church more than in past days. Each of these is a correction, and a salutary one. 2K theology has at times tended toward an unhealthy isolationism; Kuyperianism has at times tended toward an uncareful "redeem culture" approach. On a personal level, but also a broader one, I am thankful to see the two groups finding increasing commonality. This book represents encouraging progress toward that end.

The major point of agreement today among many evangelical believers is this: our duty is to be faithful, biblical, and steady. The New Testament does not call us to renew the world by our own work. We are to plunge into this present darkness and work with abandon to speak truth and act in love (Matt 22:34–39). But only Christ can put the world to rights. Only Christ can call the nations to bow at his feet. Only Christ can overcome the devil, consign him to undying flame, and end his reign of terror. Only Christ can usher in the world of love, to use Jonathan Edwards's beautiful descriptor of our eschatological home. Only Christ can; only Christ shall.

Until that day, we wait. We may see God work in amazing ways in our neighborhood, city, or country. God is not limited; God is not small. But in general, Christians are not walking the way of earthly glory. We are walking the way of the cross. We are following a crucified and resurrected Savior who has ascended to the Father's right hand. We live in triumph already, triumph won by the work of Christ on our behalf, but that triumph is not yet realized as it will be on the last day.

Second Corinthians 4:7–10 speaks powerfully to our current station. It does not ring out with the promise of cultural conquest. Instead, it urges us to persevere in bitterly difficult circumstances:

> But we have this treasure in jars of clay, to show that the surpassing power belongs to God and not to us. We are afflicted in every way, but not crushed; perplexed, but not driven to despair; persecuted, but not forsaken; struck down, but not destroyed; always carrying in the body the death of Jesus, so that the life of Jesus may also be manifested in our bodies.

The last day is indeed coming. But it is not here now. So, until then, we persevere. We groan. We pray. We weep. We rejoice. We endure. We fight evil. By the grace of God, we stay steady in Jesus Christ. The tomb is empty; the gospel is advancing; very soon, the Son will make all the sad things untrue.

Come, Lord Jesus.

Dr. Owen Strachan
Provost, Grace Bible Theological Seminary
Author, *The War on Men* and *Christianity and Wokeness*

INTRODUCTION

A Christian doesn't have to read news headlines for very long today before becoming depressed. Society seems to be quickly plummeting further and further away from anything that even approximates justice and righteousness. We live in days of despair, threat of war, violence, murder, poverty, sickness, abortion, waning morality, injustice, and racial tensions.

But, contrary to what we might think, this is nothing new. Listen to what J. C. Ryle wrote in 1867:

> I doubt much whether there ever was a time in the history of our country, when the horizon on all sides, both political and ecclesiastical, was so thoroughly black and lowering. In every direction we see men's hearts failing for fear, and for looking for those things that seem coming on the earth. Everything around us seems unscrewed, loosened and out of joint. The fountains of the great deep appear to be breaking up. Ancient institutions are tottering, and ready to fall. Social and ecclesiastical systems are failing and crumbling away. Church and state seem alike convulsed to their very foundations, and what the end of this convulsion may be no man can tell.

That was 1867.

In bleak times such as these, it is natural to ask, "Why have things gotten so bad?" And it is also good for Christians to consider, "How then should we live?"

However, what also often happens during times of societal decay is that some Christians begin to point fingers at other Christians they believe are to blame for such decay.

Conservative Christians have long been charged with being too critical of culture, too separated, and too uninvolved in cultural engagement. In contrast to what many evangelicals have condemned as the "Christ Against Culture" posture of conservative Christians, the dominant perspective that has emerged since the rise of the New Evangelicalism in the 1950s and even come to be described by Russell Moore as "evangelical consensus"[1] is cultural transformationalism, often described as Neo-Kuyperianism or Neo-Calvinism. Although each of these movements have slightly different emphases and underlying theological rationale, several key underlying theological ideas remain consistent.

First, cultural transformationalism is based in the idea that God intends to redeem, not just elect individuals, but all creation, at least in part during the present age. "The Christian message," Carl Henry argued, "aims

---

[1] Russell Moore, *The Kingdom of Christ: The New Evangelical Perspective* (Wheaton: Crossway, 2004).

at a re-created society."[2] Transformationalism's philosophy of culture engagement is centered in soteriology, and thus language of cultural "redemption" is at its heart.

Second, transformationalism derives from the belief that God's mission and the church's mission are one and the same. The so-called *missio Dei*, the idea that God desires to redeem all creation, is the basis for understanding the church's mission in transformationalist thinking. In essence, the Great Commission is simply a continuation for the present age of what they call the "cultural mandate" of Genesis 1:28.[3] This is often framed in language of "Creation-Fall-Redemption," a description of both God's mission in history and the church's mission in culture. Christ is presently ruling all things as King, they argue, and it is part of the mission of the church to extend that rule into all spheres of society, including culture. They love to quote Abraham Kuyper's well-known statement, "There is not a square inch in the whole domain of our human existence over which Christ, who is Sovereign over *all*, does not cry: 'Mine!'"[4] in support of their view.

As such, cultural transformationalism insists that

---

[2] Carl F. H. Henry, *The Uneasy Conscience of Modern Fundamentalism*, Originally published in 1947; reprinted (Grand Rapids: Wm. B. Eerdmans Publishing, 2003), 84.

[3] See Russell Moore, *Onward: Engaging the Culture Without Losing the Gospel* (Nashville: B&H Publishing, 2015), 84.

[4] Abraham Kuyper, "Sphere Sovereignty," in *Abraham Kuyper: A Centennial Reader*, ed. James D. Bratt (Grand Rapids: Wm. B. Eerdmans, 1998), 488. Emphasis original.

"the church *qua* church must engage the social and political structures."[5] Because evangelical transformationalists believe the church to be an earthly physical manifestation of the kingdom, they see a distinctive social mandate as inherent in the church's mission. Furthermore, transformationalists tend to minimize any distinction between the mission of the church as a gathered, organized institution and individual Christians in society.

One particular form transformationalism has taken in recent days is what has come to be called "Christian Nationalism." This moniker means more than simply a nation that upholds values consistent with God's moral law or an emphasis upon Christians actively applying their biblical values to how they vote and what they support politically. As I will explain in this book, the Bible clearly teaches that we Christians ought to actively live out our biblical values in the public sphere, opposing sin and promoting righteousness.

But among those who are writing and speaking on the issue, Christian Nationalism means something more than that. Christian Nationalism is the idea that Christians ought to pursue the formation of nations that explicitly consider themselves to be Christian and govern themselves accordingly.

For example, to quote Stephen Wolfe's *The Case for Christian Nationalism,*

---

[5] Moore, *The Kingdom of Christ*, 139.

> Christian Nationalism is a totality of national action, consisting of civil laws and social customs, conducted by a Christian nation as a Christian nation, in order to procure for itself both earthly and heavenly good in Christ.[6]

"In Christian Nationalism," Wolfe goes on to say, "the nation is conscious of itself as a Christian nation and acts for itself as a Christian nation."[7] This doesn't mean that every individual in a "Christian nation" is a Christian. Wolfe is quick to acknowledge that "a nation has no power in itself to bring anyone internally to true faith—to realize heavenly good in individuals."[8] In other words, the aim is making the *nation* "Christian" *externally* with the goal that this will both bless the nation and help the individuals of that nation come to personal faith through the gospel of Jesus Christ. It strikes me that, in essence, Christian nationalists want to apply a Presbyterian theology of baptism to whole nations.

And indeed, Christian nationalists often talk about our mandate to "baptize nations." Or to put it in the words of Andrew Torba and Andrew Isker, Christian Nationalism is Christians "taking dominion and discipling nations."[9] This emphasis is expanded with what Doug

---

[6] Stephen Wolfe, *The Case for Christian Nationalism* (Moscow, ID: Canon Press, 2022), 9.
[7] Wolfe, *Christian Nationalism*, 14.
[8] Wolfe, *Christian Nationalism*, 15.
[9] Andrew Torba and Andrew Isker, *Christian Nationalism: A*

Wilson has called "mere Christendom," meaning "a network of nations bound together by a formal, public, civic acknowledgment of the Lordship of Jesus Christ, and the fundamental truth of the Apostles' Creed."[10]

In essence, this is the establishment of "cultural Christianity," which Wolfe suggests,

> implicitly orders people to the Christian faith, though it cannot bring anyone to faith. Though not a spiritual force, it does remove hindrances to faith by making Christianity plausible, and it socializes people into religious practices in which one hears the gospel.[11]

There are a variety of reasons for this emphasis in focus on Christian Nationalism and even postmillennial theonomy that are certainly understandable. The rapid rise of atrocities like "drag queen story hour," gay "marriage," LGBTQ+ distortions, and Satan worship on prime time TV have led many Christian to aggressively call for the application of Mosaic law to the nation and loudly proclaim that Christian Nationalism is the only way to beat back the onslaught of pagan secularism.

I share all of the concerns of these advocates for cultural transformation and even much of what they offer as

---

Biblical Guide for Taking Dominion and Discipling Nations (Gab AI, Inc., 2022).

[10] Douglas Wilson, *Mere Christendom* (Moscow, ID: Canon Press, 2023), 69. For a full review of Wilson's book, see the Appendix.

[11] Wolfe, *Christian Nationalism*, 28.

solutions such as active engagement in the public square, bold condemnation of immorality in society, and intentional pursuit of moral laws such as those that would abolish abortion.

However, I have grown concerned that the underlying emphases and theological basis for what transformationalists are advocating does not match what Scripture commands for the church today. What they advocate, I fear, threatens to undermine the pilgrim character of New Testament Christianity and the spiritual mission given to the church of making disciples.

On the other hand, I am equally concerned by evangelical elites who advocate for a more privatized faith, ironically with the same goal of cultural transformation. The transformationalist philosophy of influential individuals like Russell Moore and David French involve, not Christian Nationalism, but a form of Christian integrationism that seeks to "transform" the culture by attempting to gain the culture's respect so as to win positions of power among the cultural elites. Though their methodologies appear to differ, both groups are attempting to impose what they believe to be the essence of Christ's kingdom on the unbelieving world now.

I believe that Scripture teaches contrary to both of these postures. As I will argue in this book, the New Testament portrays us as citizens of the common kingdoms of this earth, but we are ultimately exiles since we are more profoundly citizens of Christ's redemptive kingdom. God has established both of these "kingdoms" as means through which he sovereignly rules all things between Adam's sin and the Second Adam's coming to reign. This means that we have responsibilities both as citizens of earthly kingdoms and as citizens of the redemptive kingdom. Understanding the biblical relationship between these two provides a very clear framework for preventing churches from losing their biblical mission while at the same time discipling Christians to actively engage in society around them.

What the Bible prescribes for us in this present age is Christian faithfulness in both realms of God's sovereign rule until Jesus the King comes again to reign forever.

1

GOD'S TWO KINGDOMS

At the heart of our philosophy of the church's responsibility toward culture is a proper understanding of how God rules sovereignly over all things, how he specifically rules his redeemed people—particularly how the New Testament church, and how his rule will culminate in the future. Another way of saying this is that central to a biblical philosophy of cultural engagement is how Scripture uses language like "rule," "reign," and "kingdom" to describe God's plan in history, and essential to this understanding is recognition that Scripture uses these kinds of "kingdom" terms to describe a couple different concepts in God's working out of his sovereign plan.

I'll summarize what I mean here and then develop it. Sometimes Scripture uses "kingdom" terminology as a metaphor to describe God's universal sovereign rule over all. Other times Scripture uses "kingdom" language as a metaphor to describe his redemptive rule over his people. And other times Scripture describes a very concrete, literal kingdom on earth. Exploring these three uses of kingdom language in God's plan will help us understand our relationship to each.

THE UNIVERSAL REIGN OF GOD

First, there is one clear sense in which the Bible refers to a kingdom that is eternal and universal in scope. The psalmist proclaims, "The Lord has established his throne in the heavens, and his kingdom rules over all" (Ps 103:19) and "Your kingdom is an everlasting kingdom, and your dominion endures throughout all generations" (Ps 145:13). All aspects of the universe fall under this rule, including what we might commonly consider culture: social and family structures, government, agriculture, the arts, and so forth. God rules it all.

Within this universal reign, God created Adam in his image. God is the sovereign king, but Adam was made in God's image to be a vice-regent who would rule over all creation on God's behalf:

> So God created man in his own image, in the image of God he created him; male and female he created them. [28] And God blessed them. And God said to them, "Be fruitful and multiply and fill the earth and subdue it, and have dominion over the fish of the sea and over the birds of the heavens and over every living thing that moves on the earth." (Gen 1:27-28)

This was a blessing given to Adam as a representative of all humanity to take the raw materials of God's creation and use them for his glory and their good; this is essentially what we call culture—what we make of God's creation. This blessing establishes the basis for common human institutions such as marriage, family, agriculture, horticulture, and husbandry.

It was a blessing, but it was also a responsibility. "Subdue" and "have dominion" are royal terms, the former term later used to describe Israel's subduing of the land of Canaan (Num 32:22, 29; Josh 18:1), and the latter term used to describe the Messiah's future reign (Ps 110:2). Made in God's image, man is given the role of God's regal representative on earth. As Eugene Merrill notes, "Man is created to reign in a manner that demonstrates his lordship, his domination (by force if necessary) over all creation."[1] God is sovereign king over all creation, but he formed man in his image to be his vice-regent on earth.

Also important to note here is that God gives this dominion to *all* human beings, not just believers; this blessing occurs before the Fall. All humans have been blessed with dominion over creation, and thus God rules his universal kingdom through all people created in his image.

The realm of this kingdom over which man was to rule as God's regal representative was a garden God planted as his earthly palace (Gen 2:8). God placed the man whom he had formed in his palace, adorned it with rich food and gold, and put Adam to work: "The Lord God

---

[1] Eugene H. Merrill, "A Theology of the Pentateuch," in *A Biblical Theology of the Old Testament*, ed. Roy B. Zuck (Chicago: Moody Publishers, 1991), 15.

took the man and put him in the garden of Eden to work it and keep it" (Gen 2:15).

Yet here the language shifts from royal language to priestly language, revealing a second role man was to play in the garden realm. The phrase "work it and keep it" signifies much more than the duties of a gardener; rather, the first verb "work" is "used frequently for spiritual service, specifically serving the Lord (Deut. 4:19) and for the duties of the Levites (see Num. 3:7-8; 4:23-24, 26)." The second verb "keep" has a "religious use . . . of observing spiritual duties or keeping the commands (Lev. 18:4). It also is used for the duty of the Levites to guard the tabernacle (cf. Num 1:53; 3:7-8)." Allen Ross explains,

> In places where these two verbs are found together, they often refer to the duties of the Levites (cf. Num. 3:7-8; 8:26; 18:5-6), keeping the laws of God (especially in the sanctuary service) and offering spiritual service in the form of the sacrifices and all the related duties—serving the LORD, safeguarding his commands, and guarding the sanctuary from the intrusion of anything profane or evil.[2]

In other words, the four verbs in Genesis 2 that describe man's purpose in the garden indicate that God created man to be his kingly representative and his priestly

---

[2] Allen P. Ross, *Recalling the Hope of Glory: Biblical Worship from the Garden to the New Creation* (Grand Rapids: Kregel, 2006), 105-6.

representative. The garden was not only God's earthly palace, but also his earthly temple. God was present with his people in the sanctuary as he "walked" with them in the cool of the garden (Gen 3:8). Notably, the verb for "walked" in Genesis 3:8 is used later to describe God's presence in the tabernacle (Lev 26:12; 2 Sam 7:6-7). Man was supposed to "keep" the palace-sanctuary, that is, to guard and protect its holiness, preventing those who would attempt to usurp God's reign and defile his temple.

Thus, what God intended for man in the garden was that he serve as a perfect king/priest within what Meredith Kline describes as a "holy theocracy," a perfect union between kingdom and temple, between reigning and worshiping.[3] God intended for his universal sovereign rule to be expressed through humanity in a single earthly kingdom/temple; he intended a perfect union between the cultural and the religious to exist in the garden—Adam was supposed to be the perfect king/priest. Had Adam succeeded in this responsibility, mankind would have continued to perfectly rule the natural world as mediators of God's universal rule.

This is what David was referring to when he said in Psalm 8:4-8,

> What is man that you are mindful of him,
>   and the son of man that you care for him?

---

[3] Meredith G. Kline, *Kingdom Prologue: Genesis Foundations for a Covenantal Worldview* (Eugene, OR: Wipf and Stock, 2006), 157.

⁵ Yet you have made him a little lower than the
>heavenly beings
>and crowned him with glory and honor.
⁶ You have given him dominion over the works of your
>hands;
>you have put all things under his feet,
⁷ all sheep and oxen,
>and also the beasts of the field,
⁸ the birds of the heavens, and the fish of the sea,
>whatever passes along the paths of the seas.

God chose to rule his world through man.

However, we know what happened. When the author of Hebrews quotes that passage from Psalm 8, which claims that God has put everything under the feet of man, he says in the next verse, "At present, we do not yet see everything in subjection to him" (Heb 2:8). Adam failed. He disobeyed God's command to have dominion over creation; he allowed a creature, the serpent, to be king. He failed to guard God's garden sanctuary and allowed Satan to defile it. As the representative of all humankind, Adam failed to be God's perfect king/priest, and he was exiled from the palace/sanctuary of God's presence.

Adam's failure did not end the universal sovereign reign of God, of course, and many of the passages in Scripture that speak of God ruling over all refer to that continual, never-ending reign of God on his throne. All of this was part of God's sovereign plan.

But Adam's failure did result in a curse. God pronounced a curse upon Adam and Eve and all creation. However, in the midst of his curse upon the serpent, he provided a glimmer of hope in Genesis 3:15:

> I will put enmity between you and the woman, and between your offspring and her offspring; he shall bruise your head, and you shall bruise his heel.

God promised that one day a seed of the woman—a Second Adam—would accomplish what the First Adam failed to do. He would crush the usurper's head and cleanse the defiled sanctuary, fulfilling the God-given role of the perfect king/priest.

Yet that did not happen right away, of course. Roughly four thousand years separate God's promise of a Second Adam and the his appearance. God could have left humankind in chaos during that entire time, and in fact, he did for a while. As we read in Genesis 6:5-7,

> The Lord saw that the wickedness of man was great in the earth, and that every intention of the thoughts of his heart was only evil continually. [6] And the Lord regretted that he had made man on the earth, and it grieved him to his heart. [7] So the Lord said, "I will blot out man whom I have created from the face of the land, man and animals and creeping things and birds of the heavens, for I am sorry that I have made them."

In summary, God intended for there to be one kingdom/temple on earth, an expression of his sovereign rule over all things that was a union between man's dominion over creation—that is, *culture*—and man's relationship with God—that is, *religion*. Adam failed the requirements to rule that one kingdom, and so between his failure and the Second Adam's success, God separated the two aspects of his united kingdom into two realms of his sovereign rule.

THE COMMON KINGDOM

In the interim, between the First Adam's failure and the Second Adam's success, the curse resulted in a separation between kingdom and worship. First, God provided a means of stability and peace for the kingdoms of the earth. In the midst of his common curse upon all, Kline notes that "common grace was introduced to act as a rein to hold in check the curse on mankind, and to make possible an interim historical environment as the theater for a program of redemption."[4] Even after Cain murdered Abel, God promised preservation of justice to this unrighteous man, implying the establishment of legal systems that would prevent unbridled evil in the world (Gen 4:13-16). And indeed, Cain built a common grace city where that measure of justice was maintained (Gen 4:17).

God further established other common grace

---

[4] Kline, *Kingdom Prologue*, 155.

institutions through which he works providentially to preserve peace and order in societies filled with depraved people. Before the fall, he had already established the institution of marriage—and by extension, family—as one of the fundamental building blocks of human society and one of the central common grace human institutions he would use to cultivate and preserve order and flourishing in his world (Gen 2:18-24). After the fall, the family continued to be an institution of blessing for all people (Gen 4:17-22). The work that God had established in the garden as a blessing for mankind, though now cursed because of sin, continued for all mankind as a means of prosperity, including the development of husbandry, the arts, and metallurgy (Gen 4:20-22).

Further, God formally instituted human government as another common grace means for maintaining a semblance of order in what, left to themselves, would be chaotic societies. God formally established human government in Genesis 9. This text occurs just after that significant illustration in Genesis 6-8 of rebellion of humankind against the rule of God and God's judgment of that rebellion through a worldwide flood. After Noah and his family were saved in the ark and finally stood again on dry land, this is what happened:

> And God blessed Noah and his sons and said to them, "Be fruitful and multiply and fill the earth. ² The fear of you and the dread of you shall be upon every beast

of the earth and upon every bird of the heavens, upon everything that creeps on the ground and all the fish of the sea. Into your hand they are delivered. ³ Every moving thing that lives shall be food for you. And as I gave you the green plants, I give you everything. ⁴ But you shall not eat flesh with its life, that is, its blood. ⁵ And for your lifeblood I will require a reckoning: from every beast I will require it and from man. From his fellow man I will require a reckoning for the life of man.

⁶ "Whoever sheds the blood of man, by man shall his blood be shed, for God made man in his own image.

⁷ And you, be fruitful and multiply, increase greatly on the earth and multiply in it." (Gen 9:1-7)

God's covenant with Noah in Genesis 9 reveals God's plan to preserve humankind and creation until the Second Adam establishes his rule. First, notice that in his covenant with Noah, God specifically repeats the blessings of Genesis 1:28—"Be fruitful and multiply and fill the earth." He wants humans to continue to engage in cultural matters like having children and working the ground—this is a blessing because it helps to maintain order in the world.

But notice that he does not repeat the command to have dominion. That command was given to Adam as our representative, and he failed as our representative. *We* failed in him. Sinful humanity will never be able to exercise dominion over creation—we need a perfect man to do that for us. Our work in culture is simply a way to maintain order as a blessing to us until the Second Adam takes dominion.

And also, because of the presence of sin, in God's covenant with Noah he established additional measures by which in his providence he would preserve the stability of a cursed world. He promised that he would never again judge the world with a worldwide flood—he will providentially preserve nature. And he also established the earthly institution of human government, with its God-given responsibility of capital punishment: "Whoever sheds the blood of man, by man shall his blood be shed, for God made man in his own image." God gave this responsibility to govern the world and its people once again to all humankind as a means through which God would sovereignly control man's sinfulness and preserve the world and its order until the Second Adam would establish his reign as the perfect king/priest.

Thus even pagan magistrates can enforce God's moral law involving peaceful relations between citizens since they are still made in God's image (though marred by sin), "the law is written on their hearts" (Rom 2:15), and by God's common grace (Matt 5:45), even unbelievers often recognize that society simply works better when certain morality is enforced. This is still God's kingdom, and so human authorities are supposed to govern on his behalf and according to his rules as a way to maintain stability in a sin-cursed world.

In other words, the regal aspect of Adam's garden role continues imperfectly for all humankind as a common grace means to imperfectly preserve a degree of order and peace until Christ establishes his perfect theocratic Kingdom on earth. This is what we might call the common kingdom of God—this kingdom is not redemptive in nature, and it is not limited only to redeemed people; the common kingdom is God's providential rule over all through human institutions that he has appointed to maintain order in this world.

THE REDEMPTIVE KINGDOM

However, God also called out a subset from among the common kingdoms as a worshiping community. This distinction between two subsets of humanity was declared already in the promise of Genesis 3:15 when God declared that there would be enmity between Satan's offspring and the woman's offspring. When it comes to worship, only two options exist: Christ or Antichrist. There is no neutral middle ground—individuals worship either Christ or Satan, and thus there exists a spiritual antithesis between believers and unbelievers for all of human history. This enmity was manifested immediately after the Fall with Cain and Abel. Abel drew near to God in worship through the sacrificial means God prescribed, thus demonstrating righteous fidelity to the woman's offspring (Heb 11:4). Cain "was of the evil one and murdered his brother . . . because his own deeds were evil and his brother's righteous" (1 Jn 3:12).

Unlike within the common grace institutions of the world, where all humans share a measure of commonality, God's worshiping community is set apart from unbelieving humanity. God called out Noah and his family as a redeemed cultic community, saving them from the judgment that fell upon the rest of wicked humanity. In God's covenant with Abraham (Gen 17:1-8), God called out a redeemed people for his name. As exemplified by Abel, Noah, and Abraham, the requirement for redemption and membership in this cultic community is faith—"By faith Abel offered to God a more acceptable sacrifice than Cain" (Heb 11:4); "by faith Noah . . . constructed an ark for the saving of his household" (Heb 11:7); and Abraham "believed the Lord, and he counted it to him as righteousness" (Gen 15:6).

Abraham and his family were a called-out worshiping community. And as such, though they were part of the common kingdoms of the world, they were sojourners and pilgrims. Abraham sought "the city that has foundations, whose designer and builder is God" (Heb 11:10). God's redeemed people, though still sharing commonalities with the rest of humanity, are nevertheless "strangers and exiles on the earth," since "they desire a better country, that is, a heavenly one" (Heb 11:13, 16).

Their temporal citizenship is in earthly cities, but their religious identity is in a heavenly kingdom.

In redeeming this called out community, God also established the means by which the Second Adam would come and earn the right to rule, *and* the means by which citizens would be gathered into his perfect kingdom. This is the second way Scripture often uses "kingdom" language: to refer to God's specific rule through the Second Adam over his redeemed people. The foundation for this kingdom is found in God's covenant with Abraham in Genesis 17:

> When Abram was ninety-nine years old the Lord appeared to Abram and said to him, "I am God Almighty; walk before me, and be blameless, ² that I may make my covenant between me and you, and may multiply you greatly." ³ Then Abram fell on his face. And God said to him, ⁴ "Behold, my covenant is with you, and you shall be the father of a multitude of nations. ⁵ No longer shall your name be called Abram, but your name shall be Abraham, for I have made you the father of a multitude of nations. ⁶ I will make you exceedingly fruitful, and I will make you into nations, and kings shall come from you. ⁷ And I will establish my covenant between me and you and your offspring after you throughout their generations for an everlasting covenant, to be God to you and to your offspring after you. ⁸ And I will give to you and to your

offspring after you the land of your sojournings, all the land of Canaan, for an everlasting possession, and I will be their God."

God's covenant with Abraham accomplished three important things. First, in this covenant, God formally established his redemptive kingdom in which he distinguished his chosen people from the rest of the human race. He promised to make of Abraham's descendants a great nation, and that through this great chosen nation, "all the nations of the earth will be blessed" (Gen 18:18, 22:18, 26:4, 28:14). But unlike the common kingdom, this Kingdom is reserved only for redeemed people. As exemplified by Abraham himself, the requirement for redemption and citizenship in this Kingdom is faith—Abraham "believed the Lord, and he counted it to him as righteousness" (Gen 15:6). These citizens of God's redemptive kingdom would be set apart from the other citizens of the common kingdom, illustrated through circumcision.

Second, God's covenant with Abraham also established the specific family from which the Second Adam would come—"kings shall come from you." God will make a covenant with one of those anointed kings, David, that *the Anointed King* would come through his line.

And indeed, the Second Adam came in the person of Jesus Christ, God's Son, who perfectly fulfilled the role of God's king/priest. Like with the first Adam, the serpent tempted Jesus and tried to usurp his rule, but Jesus conquered him. Like with the first Adam, God appointed Jesus to be a priest, and Jesus perfectly obeyed by cleansing the temple and offering up himself as an atoning sacrifice. Unlike the first Adam, Jesus passed the test and earned the right to rule as the perfect king/priest, and after his resurrection from the dead, he ascended into the heavenly palace/temple itself, where he sat down at the right hand of God's throne. Christ succeeded where Adam failed and is now enjoying the blessings Adam never attained.

So when Scripture uses kingdom language with reference to the redeemed people of God under the rule of Christ, the perfect king/priest, it is different from God's universal common kingdom. This redemptive kingdom does not include all humankind; it includes only those who place their faith in this perfect king/priest, "sons of the kingdom" (Matt 13:38) who have been delivered "from the domain of darkness and transferred . . . to the kingdom of his beloved Son, in whom we have redemption, the forgiveness of sin" (Col 1:13).

TWO KINGDOMS

This establishes the reality of two kingdoms: (1) a universal common kingdom, God's sovereign superintendence over all things—including creation and human institutions, cultures, and societies, and (2) a redemptive kingdom, God's specific rule over his redeemed people. God's covenant with Noah established the common kingdom, and God's covenant with Abraham established the redemptive kingdom. The common kingdom includes all humanity and involves family, government, cultural pursuits, and earthly vocations. The redemptive kingdom includes only those who submit to the King and involves a redemptive relationship with God. The common kingdom involves temporal, physical matters. The redemptive kingdom involves spiritual matters.

PROMISE OF FUTURE UNION

Because of Adam's failure, these two kingdoms are at this present time distinct, but God intends one day to unite them into one Kingdom. This is the third, and perhaps most concrete way Scripture uses "kingdom" terminology: it prophesies the reign of a perfect King in which he will unite God's universal reign with his redemptive reign, a day when "the earth shall be full of the knowledge of the Lord as the waters cover the sea" (Isa 11:9), when Christ will "have dominion from sea to sea, and from River to the ends of the earth" (Ps 72:8).

God has always intended for the common and the redemptive to be united in one perfect Kingdom. In God's providence, Adam's failure prevented that, but the Old Testament prophets continued to promise it, such Daniel:

And in the days of those kings the God of heaven will

set up a kingdom that shall never be destroyed, nor shall the kingdom be left to another people. It shall break in pieces all these kingdoms and bring them to an end, and it shall stand forever. (Dan 2:44)

But notice also that although Christ has already established his rule over his redeemed people, as Hebrews 2:8 says, "At present, we do not yet see everything in subjection to him." Christ is, as Psalm 110 states, presently seated at the Father's right hand until the Father makes his enemies his footstool. The perfect eternal Kingdom has been promised and ensured, but it is not yet a complete reality. It will happen only after Jesus comes again, when "the kingdom of this world"—that is, the common kingdom—"will become the kingdom of our Lord and of his Christ" (Rev 11:15).

MODEL FOR FUTURE UNION

In the Old Testament, however, God did foreshadow what this union would look like. The third thing accomplished in the Abrahamic Covenant by God choosing this one family was the establishment of a nation that would serve as both a prototype of the united Kingdom of God and further evidence that sinful humans could not achieve it. In other words, God chose the nation of Israel to be a model of the union between the universal common kingdom and the redemptive kingdom.

By means of the Mosaic covenant, Israel became a proto-typical theocratic union of kingdom and worship. The Mosaic Law given at Mt. Sinai united redemptive qualifications with moral and civil in which the Law governed every aspect of their society. This was an earthly picture of what the united universal redemptive kingdom would look like.

However, even though Israel as a nation was a union of kingdom and worship, it is important to recognize that the two were still distinct in a significant sense, made clear by the fact that no one leader held authority over both kingdom and worship. God established political leaders (judges and kings) to rule the kingdom and priests to lead the worship. And because of Israel's continual rebellion, idolatry, and eventually indifference, God terminated that united kingdom when his Shekinah-Glory departed from the temple in Ezekiel 11.

Christ's first coming qualified him as the perfect king/priest and accomplished the means of redeeming a people who would comprise the citizenship of the universal redemptive Kingdom, but Christ's first coming never brings with it the same union of the civil and redemptive that existed in either the Garden of Eden or Israel's kingdom. Christ preached this kingdom while he is on earth, and he promised that it will come. But this concrete, literal kingdom that unites the universal common kingdom with the redemptive kingdom, according to Christ in John 18:36 "is not of this world"—that union is not a present reality. It will happen only after Jesus comes again and all things are in subjection to him.

The book of Hebrews addresses both kingdom and worship in this present age. First, the author quotes God's declaration in Psalm 8 that he intends for man to exercise regal dominion over all the earth; however, "At present, we do not yet see everything in subjection to him" (Heb 2:8). The First Adam failed, and still all things are not yet in subjection to the son of man. But, "because of the suffering of death," Jesus is "crowned with glory and honor" (Heb 2:9)—he has earned the right to rule; Christ is, as Psalm 110 states, presently seated at the Father's right hand until the Father makes his enemies his footstool. The perfect eternal kingdom has been promised and already ensured, but it is not yet a complete reality. Christ presently rules over his redeemed people, but the consummation of his rule over all things on earth will happen when he comes again, when "the kingdom of this world"—that is, the common grace kingdom—"will become the kingdom of our Lord and of his Christ" (Rev 11:15).

In other words, we should not expect a union of the common kingdom and the redemptive kingdom in this present age. It will happen in the age to come.

HOW THEN SHALL WE LIVE?

This biblical understanding of the two kingdoms of God

and their future union has several important implications for our lives as Christians and for our church ministry and our relationship to the world around us, which I will expand in the following chapters.

First, Adam failed to be the king/priest God commanded him to be, and since we were in Adam, we will never be able to be what he was supposed to be. We are not new Adams who are supposed to do what Adam failed to do by somehow exercising dominion over creation.

Rather, point two, Christ is the last Adam. *He* accomplished what Adam failed to do, and *he* will exercise dominion over all creation when he comes again. To believe that it is somehow our responsibility to do what Adam failed to do would be to distrust the sufficiency of what Christ accomplished. It is not up to us to somehow "extend his reign"; Christ will do that, not us.

Third, we cannot do what Adam failed to do, but we who are redeemed—we who are in Christ—do get to inherit the perfect kingdom Adam never achieved.

> For if, because of one man's trespass, death reigned through that one man, much more will those who receive the abundance of grace and the free gift of righteousness reign in life through the one man Jesus Christ. (Rom 5:17)

Because Christ rose from the dead, we who are in him will rise from the dead, because he has been glorified, we will be glorified, and since Christ reigns in glory, we who are in him "will also reign with him" (2 Tim 2:12).

But not yet; not until Jesus comes again. Paul says in 1 Corinthians 15:22-25,

> For as in Adam all die, so also in Christ shall all be made alive. ²³ But each in his own order: Christ the firstfruits, then at his coming those who belong to Christ. ²⁴ Then comes the end, when he delivers the kingdom to God the Father after destroying every rule and every authority and power. ²⁵ For he must reign until he has put all his enemies under his feet.

God is currently putting Christ's enemies under his feet; when he is finished, the end will come, and then Christ will share his reign with we who believe in him.

Fourth, until he comes again, we believers live on this earth, pursuing various cultural endeavors, our jobs, participation in government, etc. in response to the fact that Christ has already done what Adam failed to do, not in an attempt to achieve what Adam failed to do. Nor should we expect the sort of Christianization of culture promised for the messianic kingdom to take place in this present age. That's not going to happen until Jesus comes again.

As I will flesh out in the chapters to follow, we Christians absolutely should do good to all people, we should work hard in the vocations to which God has called us, we should rear children who love and obey God, we should stand up against injustice when we see it, we should be engaged in politics to help restrain evil in this world—but we should not feel the weight of trying to do what Adam failed to do.

Christ has already done it! We live and work in this present age out of a response to what Christ has accomplished, looking forward to that day when he will complete it—when he will completely destroy his enemies and take dominion over all. During the present age, we live faithful and holy lives in the culture, and we pursue more kingdom citizens through bold proclamation of the gospel until the day when we will enjoy Christ's eternal kingdom, ruling and reigning with him.

2

DUAL CITIZENS

In the last chapter, we focused on the biblical reality of God's two kingdoms. After Adam failed to be the perfect king/priest that God intended him to be, ruling over the kingdom of this world and guarding the sanctuary, God promised that one day a Second Adam would come who would succeed where Adam failed. In the meantime, God separated the common kingdom from the redemptive kingdom into two kingdoms. God still rules both of these realms, but he administers his rule in different ways.

God established the common kingdom in his covenant with Noah, and he established his redemptive kingdom in his covenant with Abraham. Old Testament Israel provided a picture of what a future union of the two kingdoms would look like, and the Second Adam did come and earn the right to rule, but the union of the two kingdoms will not occur until after God has put all things under the perfect king/priest's feet and Jesus comes again. Until that day, God still rules his world in these two realms—a common realm, and a redemptive realm.

What does this mean, then, for redeemed people of God living in this present age? How ought we conduct ourselves in this present world, considering that we are still part of the common kingdom, but we also have a new identity as citizens of the redemptive kingdom? How should we relate to the culture of the world in which we live? This is particularly relevant when we understand the present reality of God's two kingdoms—if our responsibility toward culture is not dominion, what is it?

We live in a day in which most people consider culture to be neutral. Whether it is the music we listen to in our homes, the clothes we wear, the movies we watch, or the food we eat, most people today—including Christians—believe that there is nothing intrinsically moral about any cultural activity.

The problem with discussions of culture today, however, is that our contemporary idea of culture comes from secular anthropologists who came up with the idea of culture as a way to explain the differences between people groups that would not judge the way that these different groups behave. You won't find the term *culture* in Scripture—that idea comes from secular anthropology. Since these anthropologists believe in Darwinian evolution, they insist that each group of people on the earth evolved into what they are, and so we dare not compare or judge the various "cultures" of these people groups. We cannot place any value, they say, on how different people groups choose to live.

The question for Christians today, however, should be this: how does the Bible discuss different ways of life? When one group of people behave in a different way than another group of people, does the Bible explain these differences as neutral, or is there something deeper going on?

This is an important question because it very practically affects how we view the various cultural activities in the common kingdoms of this world. Various groups of people have different customs, dress in different ways, have different political systems, view family and children differently, and behave in different ways. We call this culture. If culture is neutral, then it really doesn't matter how you act. But if culture is not neutral, then how you behave and what you do with God's creation certainly does matter. So it is important to consider what our attitude toward culture should be, particularly in light of the reality of God's two kingdoms.

DEFINING CULTURE BIBLICALLY

New Testament authors use several terms that correspond to our contemporary notion of culture as "way of life," and one text that illustrates them well is 1 Peter 1:3–25. The most common word in the New Testament that means "way of life" or "behavior" is the word *anastrophē*. In 1 Peter 1, the ESV translates it as "conduct" in verse 15. Peter uses a verb form of the term in verse 17: "conduct yourselves." Then he uses the noun again in verse 18, where the ESV translates it as "ways," and this translation is a very good one that demonstrates how this term could be easily translated as "culture." There is one more term in this passage that has a very similar definition as *anastrophē*, and it is found in verse 17 where the ESV translates it as "deeds." This is the term *ergon*, and it has the same idea of behavior, conduct, or way of life. So again, I would suggest that it could very easily be translated as "culture."[1]

BE HOLY

What Peter says in this passage well illustrates how the New Testament—indeed, all Scripture—addresses the way of life (culture) of God's redeemed people. The central command in Peter's discourse is found in verse 15: "be holy in all your conduct"—*anastrophē*, way of life, culture.

To be holy literally means to be set apart from the regular, mundane, earthly things and be separated unto God. In the Old Testament, the Sabbath was a day set apart from every other regular day in that it was a day especially dedicated to God. Priests were separated from normal men by their dedication to God, and so forth. So this

---

[1] For a more detailed explanation of this point, see my book, Scott Aniol, *By the Waters of Babylon: Worship in a Post-Christian Culture* (Grand Rapids: Kregel Ministry, 2015).

command is to be set apart from the regular and normal things of life and be dedicated to God.

Now notice that Peter did not say here, "be righteous" or "be godly," although he certainly could have. In other words, this command is not directly addressing abstaining from sinful practices. Instead, by using the word *holy*, Peter is commanding us to be set apart even from otherwise good and normal things, and instead to be separated and dedicated to God.

So the behavior of Christians—our culture—should be distinct; it should be unique. Certainly the behavior of Christians should not be sinful, but it's more than that. The behavior of Christians (culture) should be set apart from normal, everyday behavior of unbelieving people. The culture of Christians should manifest a deep dedication and separation unto God. When we consider how we are to behave, we often focus on whether or not our behavior is sinful; we ask, "What's wrong with this?" But the thrust here is to focus not just on whether our behavior is sinful, but whether it manifests a clear distinction and separation from the values and desires of this world and a clear focus on God.

Why must there be a distinction? Because of what leads up to this command in verse 13: "Therefore, preparing your minds for action, and being sober-minded, set your hope fully on the grace that will be brought to you at the revelation of Jesus Christ." We are a redeemed people who have experienced the grace of God—we are citizens of God's redemptive kingdom. This is what the first twelve verses of Peter's letter address:

> According to his great mercy, he has caused us to be born again to a living hope through the resurrection of Jesus Christ from the dead, to an inheritance that is imperishable, undefiled, and unfading, kept in heaven for you, who by God's power are being guarded through faith for a salvation ready to be revealed in the last time.

We who are redeemed have an inheritance waiting for us; we will rule with Christ in the eternal kingdom. Therefore, we are to set our hope fully on the grace that will be brought to us when Jesus comes again. We ought to live differently from the unsaved people around us because we *are* different from them. We have a different hope because we have a different citizenship.

Peter is expressly distinguishing between Christians and the world—between believers and unbelievers. These two groups of people have different values and different desires, and therefore they have different behavior—they have different culture. And this command gives another description that illustrates this distinction—it calls Christians in verse 14 "children of obedience." The phrase is not, like a lot of translations render it, simply "obedient children," like children who are obedient. Rather, the grammatical construction is as if obedience is our mother; we are children of obedience. Obedience characterizes the essence of who we are.

This highlights the contrast between believers and unbelievers when we consider what Paul calls unbelievers in Ephesians 2:2; he calls unbelievers "children of disobedience." They are characterized by disobedience to God. The contrast is between the values of Christians and the values of non-Christians. We have different parents.

So Peter says, as people whose mother is obedience, who are characterized by obedience, we must be holy—set apart, distinct, dedicated to God—in all our behavior, our way of life, our culture. The contrast to this is what Peter says at the end of verse 14: "Do not be conformed to the former lusts which were yours in your ignorance." The opposite of being holy in your culture is to allow your culture to conform to the desires of unbelievers.

This is the reality that we often forget when we are talking about culture: there really is no such thing as neutrality. Even the sorts of desires and lifestyles of unbelievers that *look* neutral are in reality the expression of a value system that hates God and is concerned only with self. The Bible teaches that mankind is totally corrupt in their thinking, their values, and their desires. Whenever we enter a discussion of culture we must remember that there is a fundamental antithesis between the values and desires of believers and unbelievers.

This is why Peter says that we must not conform ourselves to the ways of thinking and valuing and desiring that naturally characterize unbelievers. This is the exact same language Paul uses in Romans 12:2 when he tells us not to be conformed to this world. Peter calls unbelievers here "ignorant," similarly to how Paul says in Ephesians 4:17-19 that Christians "must no longer walk as the Gentiles do, in the futility of their minds. They are darkened in their understanding, alienated from the life of God because of the ignorance [same term] that is in them, due to their hardness of heart. They have become callous and have given themselves up to sensuality, greedy to practice every kind of impurity." This is the sort of value system that characterizes unbelievers—even when they act in what seems to be good ways—and to conform ourselves to that in any way is the antithesis of what it means to be holy in our conduct.

And this is why culture—our behavior—is never neutral. What we do and how we live is a manifestation of what we value and what we believe. And so we may judge—we *must* judge cultural behavior to discern whether that behavior is fitting with biblical values and beliefs.

Ultimately, the reason we should be distinct and set apart, according to Peter, is that God himself is distinct and set apart. God is holy. And because he is holy, we must be holy. If we really have our hope set on him and his grace and on the coming of Christ instead of the pleasures of this world and the desires of unbelievers, then we will be set apart.

Many Christians today are so enamored with the world that Christians really have the same values as unbelievers. There is no distinction; there is no holiness. The entertainment of many Christians today embodies values that are exactly the same as the values of ignorant unbelievers. The music of Christians today sounds just like the music that comes from ignorant desires. The dress styles, the leisure time, the work ethic, the morals—the culture of Christians today more often than not looks no different than the culture of the unbelieving world that embodies and expresses values, desires, and beliefs that are hostile to God. There is no holiness.

EXILES

This is why a healthy understanding of God's two kingdoms is so important for us. As Peter says in verse 17, "And if you call on him as Father who judges impartially according to each one's deeds"—in other words, if you are a citizen of the redemptive kingdom, "conduct yourselves with fear throughout the time of your exile."

As believers in Jesus Christ, Christians are subjects in the redemptive rule of God—"our citizenship is in heaven" (Phil 3:20). We are "citizens with the saints and members of the household of God" (Eph 2:19), and as such, we are set apart from the unbelieving people of this world. Christians are "not of the world" just as Jesus is "not of the world" (Jn 15:19; 17:14, 16). Jesus said that this world hates him, because he "testif[ies] about it that its works are evil" (Jn 7:7). Galatians 1:4 calls this world the "present evil age." Second Corinthians 4:4 identifies the "god of this world" as one who has "blinded the minds of the unbelievers, to keep them from seeing the light of the gospel of the glory of Christ," this one whom Ephesians 2:2 calls "the prince of the power of the air, the spirit that is now at work in the sons of disobedience."

This is why Peter describes our current situation as "the time of your exile" (1 Pet 1:17) and specifically calls us "sojourners and exiles" (1 Pet 2:11). John commands Christians, "Do not love the world or the things in the world" (1 Jn 2:15), and Paul insists that Christians "do not be conformed to this world" (Rom 12:2). We have been redeemed as citizens of Christ's kingdom, and as 1 Peter 2:18 says, we have been redeemed *from* "the futile ways inherited from our forefathers." We have been redeemed *from* the sinful culture around us and redeemed *to* a new way of life as citizens of the redemptive kingdom. In other words, if we want to look to the Old Testament for an analogy to our present situation as Christians in this age, we are more like the sojourning patriarchs and the exiled Hebrews than either the Edenic or Mosaic holy theocracies.

This recognition should engender within Christians a healthy distrust in the beliefs, values, and cultural pursuits of the unbelieving world around them. Since culture—that is, systems of behavior that characterize a particular society—necessarily results from the dominant worldview, beliefs, and values of that society, it should not be surprising that much of the cultural activity of a thoroughly pagan society would be expressions of those sinful values.

We must be always suspicious that what is around us is contrary to God's law. Some of it may not be, but that should at least be our suspicion. We must keep our hope fixed on our end goal, always vigilant, girding up our minds for action, not allowing ourselves to get intoxicated with this present world. We must set our affections on things above and not on earthly things, not being conformed to this world or the passions of our former ignorance. We *should* be distinct, set apart, and holy. We should not have the same desires, tastes, preferences, and behaviors as unbelievers, because they have different values than we do. We have been redeemed from their lifestyle; we are new creatures with a new way of life—a new culture.

Christians in the first through third centuries recognized this. They couldn't help but recognize their status as exiles because they were increasingly persecuted for their faith. Yet something happened in the fourth century that led God's people to forget that they were sojourners and exiles. In 313, the Roman emperor Constantine legalized Christianity. Now, of course, that was a good thing. We Christians should never desire persecution. But then in 392, emperor Theodosius declared

Christianity to be the official religion of the Roman empire and outlawed all other religions. In essence, the church and state eventually united, forming what many call "Christendom," and church leaders literally wanted to turn the empire into a holy theocracy like Israel, climaxing in the Holy Roman Empire. This was an attempt to "redeem culture," to unite the common kingdom with the redemptive kingdom into one unified kingdom.

The problem is that God never intended this kind of union for the present age. Now, many good things came as a result of that union—much of the cultural production that came out of Christendom, for example, the art and literature and music, contain values and morals that are noble and good. Nevertheless, this union of the church with the broader culture not only created a lot of nominal Christianity, it also lulled true Christians into forgetting that they were exiles.

The Reformers, especially Martin Luther and John Calvin, argued against the church/state union by articulating a two-kingdom theology. Here is Calvin, for example:

> Therefore, in order that none of us may stumble on that stone, let us first consider that there is a twofold government in man: one aspect is spiritual, whereby the conscience is instructed in piety and in reverencing God; the second is political, whereby man is educated for the duties of humanity and citizenship that

must be maintained among men. These are usually called the "spiritual" and the "temporal" jurisdiction (not improper terms) by which is meant that the former sort of government pertains to the life of the soul, while the latter has to do with the concerns of the present life—not only with food and clothing but with laying down laws whereby a man may live his life among other men holily, honorably, and temperately. For the former resides in the inner mind, while the latter regulates only outward behavior. The one we may call the spiritual kingdom, the other, the political kingdom. Now these two, as we have divided them, must always be examined separately; and while one is being considered, we must call away and turn aside the mind from thinking about the other. There are in man, so to speak, two worlds, over which different kings and different laws have authority.[2]

However, these early Reformers were unable to completely disentangle themselves from socio-political ties during their lives. The Church of England especially, as its name indicates, maintained a close union between Church and state. It really wasn't until the early Baptists in England, and a few groups prior to Baptists, that we find a clear articulation of the need to recover a

---

[2] John Calvin, *Institutes of the Christian Religion (1536)*, trans. Ford Lewis Battles, Rev. ed. (Grand Rapids: Wm. B. Eerdmans Publishing, 1995), 3.19.15.

separation between church and state—a Baptist distinctive. This emphasis of the separation of church and state influenced the founding of the United States of America as well, but nevertheless, the effects of Christendom can still be observed today, for good and for ill.

How many Christians today consider themselves sojourners and exiles? How many Christians recognize that their citizenship is in another kingdom and that they are currently living in a world hostile to them and their way of life? How many Christians consider themselves distinct from the unbelieving people around them?

RESIDENTS

Yet this is not the complete picture of the Christian situation. The presence of sin in the world does not entirely destroy the image of God in unbelieving people, and the common grace institutions that God established to preserve order are still in effect. Even though Satan is the "god of this world," God is still on the throne of his universal kingdom, and he is still preserving his creation through families, human governments, and other God-ordained human institutions. Thus even unbelievers, when they act consistent with that order, can do what God has blessed them to do—they can preserve order and justice in the world, they devise successful political systems, they can produce worthy art, and they can teach things that are true.

And so, in these kinds of activities, God's people can stand alongside unbelieving people, participating in and contributing to society as citizens of the universal common kingdom of God. A perfect illustration of this is what the prophet Jeremiah says to Israel in Babylonian exile, a situation for Israel analogous to the church's situation in this age:

> Thus says the Lord of hosts, the God of Israel, to all the exiles whom I have sent into exile from Jerusalem to Babylon: ⁵ Build houses and live in them; plant gardens and eat their produce. ⁶ Take wives and have sons and daughters; take wives for your sons, and give your daughters in marriage, that they may bear sons and daughters; multiply there, and do not decrease. ⁷ But seek the welfare of the city where I have sent you into exile, and pray to the Lord on its behalf, for in its welfare you will find your welfare. (Jer 29:4-7)

Israel in exile experienced a stark antithesis between their religion and the religion of their captors—they sat down and wept as their captors mocked them when they gathered by the waters of Babylon to worship (Ps 137), and yet they were able to share commonality with their captors as well.

Some of the accounts of Israel in exile demonstrate this; for example, Daniel would not eat meat associated with pagan worship, refused to stop praying to Yahweh, and would not pray to the king, and yet he willingly allowed himself to be educated in the literature and language of Babylon and even served in political leadership, as did others of the people of Israel. Despite the absolute religious antithesis as members of God's redeemed people, there was much commonality between the everyday lives of the Hebrews and the everyday lives of the Babylonians with respect to the common kingdom—building houses, planting gardens, family, governing, literature, and education.

The same is true for Christians today. Jesus was clear: Render to Caesar that which is Caesar's. Why? Because the welfare of the city is also our welfare. A healthy government that protects the innocent and punishes injustice is part of God's universal reign, even if that government is pagan. In the context of teaching Christians how to live as sojourners and exiles, Peter specifically says that Christians should submit to earthly authorities and even honor them (1 Pet 2:13-18). Why? Because the welfare of the city is also our welfare. Government was instituted by God himself, and inasmuch as governing officials rule with equity and justice, they are doing exactly what God intends for them to do. Like Jeremiah, Paul commands that "supplications, prayers, intercessions, and thanksgivings be made for all people, for kings and all who are in high positions" (1 Tim 2:1-2). Why? So that "we may lead a peaceful and quiet life, godly and dignified in every way," exactly why God established human government in Genesis 9.

RESIDENT ALIENS

There is a real sense in which Christians, analogous to Israel in exile, are dual citizens—resident aliens. Christians are first and foremost citizens of the redemptive kingdom, but they are also citizens of God's universal common kingdom along with every other human being. And thus, Christians contribute to society, submit to and pray for governmental authorities, and participate in various aspects of cultural endeavors, as long as they reflect and remain consistent with God's law.

And when, as it sometimes does, the behavior of unbelievers resembles our behavior—when we garden in a similar way that they do, or when our houses look like theirs; when the way we dress or the music we listen to happens to look and sound like theirs—it is because they have adopted a way of life that happens to reflect our values, not the other way around. When this happens—because of the image of God in all people and because of God's common grace, many times unbelievers live lives that are actually *inconsistent* with what they really value and believe. They do things that actually embody and express Christian values. But the important thing here is that the similarity is not because we are copying the world; it is because they are, in a sense, borrowing from our values because things just work better when they are done in accordance with how God designed the world to work.

We should be holy and distinct from unbelieving people, but not just to be different. We behave differently than unbelievers—our culture is different than theirs—because ways of behavior are expressions of values and beliefs. And since our values and beliefs are different than theirs, our behavior is different. Even though we participate in the culture of this foreign land, our participation as worshipers of the true God should have a distinctness to it; even our garden planting and house building should have a set-apartness that characterizes it when compared to the garden planting and house building of the pagans around us.

Ultimately, our citizenship is not in this world, and therefore our way of life ought to be different from those who are. We must not be conformed to the passions of our former ignorance, but as he who called us is holy we must be holy, conducting ourselves in fear during the time of our exile, and clearly manifesting that we have set our hope on the grace that will be brought to us at the revelation of Jesus Christ.

3

REMEMBER WHO WE ARE

Our concern in this book has been how we as Christians should live in the culture around us, and we have seen that our thinking in this matter is dependent upon our understanding of how God is working in this world through two kingdoms—through a universal common kingdom, and through his redemptive kingdom. These two kingdoms are at present distinct, but they will be united when Jesus comes again.

But actually for us, the two kingdoms are not exactly distinct. The challenge for us as Christians today is that we are dual citizens—we are first and foremost citizens of God's redemptive kingdom; we have submitted ourselves to Christ's rule, and our mission is to bring others into that citizenship through evangelism and discipleship. But as human beings, we are also still citizens of God's universal common kingdom along with every other person in the world. We are living in this world as citizens, but also as exiles, very similar to how the Israelites lived in Babylon.

So while our mission as citizens of the redemptive kingdom is clear—make disciples, we still need to carefully consider what the Bible teaches about how we Christians are to live our lives as citizens and exiles in the common kingdom of this world.

Peter especially addresses us as Christians from this perspective. We have already seen that in several places Peter calls us exiles, playing on that metaphor to describe our lives as dual citizens, and in 1 Peter 2, he focuses on how we ought to live in light of this.

SOJOURNERS AND EXILES

Notice how Peter describes who we are in 1 Peter 2:9-10:

> But you are a chosen race, a royal priesthood, a holy nation, a people for his own possession, that you may proclaim the excellencies of him who called you out of darkness into his marvelous light. [10] Once you were not a people, but now you are God's people; once you had not received mercy, but now you have received mercy.

Peter is emphasizing our status as citizens of the redemptive kingdom—we are a new people for God's own possession. We are still citizens of the common kingdom, as he will focus on in a moment, but we are set apart from the other non-redeemed citizens of the common kingdom because we have received God's mercy—we are God's unique people.

In light of that reality, he begins verse 11 by describing us as "sojourners and exiles." We are resident aliens. We are in this world—God has left us here for a purpose, but in reality, this world is not our home; we're just passing through. We are sojourners and exiles.

This is important for us to remember: In a passage in which Peter is going to focus primarily on how we ought to live in God's common kingdom along with every other person on the face of the earth, he begins by reminding us of our true citizenship. The implication here is that everything about how we live in society and interact in culture must flow out of our ultimate citizenship. There is no divorcing of the sacred and "secular" for the Christian in this sense. We cannot simply say, "Well, I'm saved, heaven is my true home, Christ is going to come back one day and defeat all of his enemies, and so really nothing I do in this life matters very much. Our mission as the church is to make disciples, so we ought to just preach the gospel and go to church and not really care about anything that happens in this world."

Wrong. The whole point of Peter's book is that, in light of the fact that your citizenship is in the redemptive kingdom, in light of the fact that you are a holy nation, a people for God's own possession, you *must* live in a certain way in God's common kingdom.

So how ought we to live as sojourners and exiles?

HOW WE LIVE

Peter addresses through the rest of the book all sorts of aspects of the common kingdom of God, topics that are not unique to Christians. Let's just survey down through the book to see the kinds of issues he's about to address:

> Be subject for the Lord's sake to every human institution, whether it be to the emperor as supreme. (2:13)

> Servants, be subject to your masters with all respect, not only to the good and gentle but also to the unjust. (2:18)

> Likewise, wives, be subject to your own husbands, so that even if some do not obey the word, they may be won without a word by the conduct of their wives. (3:1)

> Do not let your adorning be external—the braiding of hair and the putting on of gold jewelry, or the clothing you wear. (3:3)

> Likewise, husbands, live with your wives in an understanding way, showing honor to the woman as the weaker vessel, since they are heirs with you of the grace of life, so that your prayers may not be hindered. (3:7)

> Finally, all of you, have unity of mind, sympathy, brotherly love, a tender heart, and a humble mind. (3:8)

Unbelievers have to deal with government, work, family, and other cultural matters as well. These are all realities of lives that God has instituted as part of the common kingdom for the common good of all humankind.

But look at what he says in verses 11 and 12, right before he moves into that discussion:

> Beloved, I urge you as sojourners and exiles to abstain from the passions of the flesh, which wage war against your soul. [12] Keep your conduct among the Gentiles honorable, so that when they speak against you as evildoers, they may see your good deeds and glorify God on the day of visitation.

Peter is about to address these topics from the perspective of people who are sojourners and exiles—we are still part of the common kingdom, but because of God's mercy now—*because we are citizens of the redemptive kingdom*, we have new beliefs and values that will impact how we live and what we do in the common kingdom.

What Peter says here in verses 11 and 12 of chapter 2 apply to everything else Peter will talk about with regard to government and family and vocation. In all of those things, we ought to be characterized as those who live by the Spirit and not according to the passions of the flesh. This sets us apart from the other citizens of the common kingdom. This makes us holy in all our conduct, as God is holy, just like Peter admonished in chapter 1.

This makes us distinct, but that distinctness is not prideful; it is not that we think we are better than all the other people of this world, so we choose to live differently than they do so that we are set apart from them.

No; we have received mercy! If not for the grace and mercy of God through Christ, we would be just like them. We are not welcome as a guest at the Table of our Lord because of something we did or some value in us that unbelievers don't have. No, "'twas the same love that spread the feast that sweetly drew us in; else we had still refused to taste, and perished in our sin" (Isaac Watts, 1707).

And not only that, this distinctness isn't to denigrate unbelieving people; it is for their good. As he says in verse 12,

> Keep your conduct among the Gentiles honorable, so that when they speak against you as evildoers, they may see your good deeds and glorify God on the day of visitation.

Jesus said something similar in Matthew 5:16, when he said, "In the same way, let your light shine before others, so that they may see your good works and give glory to your Father who is in heaven."

When we abstain from the passions of the flesh in our everyday lives alongside unbelieving people, it is not to make ourselves look better than people who are enslaved to the flesh, it is to compel unbelievers to join us in the redemptive kingdom. The term "visitation" in 1 Peter 2:12 refers to a person's redemption; it refers to when an unbeliever is convicted of his sin, responds in repentant faith, and receives pardon through Christ.

Peter brings back the same theme in chapter 3 when he discusses wives submitting to their husbands. That command applies to all wives, but notice that he is specifically addressing Christian wives who have unsaved husbands. There again Peter emphasizes the evangelistic purpose behind good conduct.

> Likewise, wives, be subject to your own husbands, so that even if some do not obey the word, they may be won without a word by the conduct of their wives, ² when they see your respectful and pure conduct. (3:1-2)

How we live in the common kingdom matters for God's glory and the good of the unbelieving people around us.

So already we can see that although our citizenships in the two kingdoms are in a sense distinct, they are also very much related. How we live in the common kingdom should be in light of our citizenship in the redemptive kingdom, and that alone serves as a witness and helps us to accomplish our mission of making disciples, of gathering more citizens into Christ's redemptive kingdom.

GOD'S TWO-FOLD REVELATION

One of the foundational truths that undergirds the reality of how God works in his two kingdoms is the nature of how he has revealed himself to people in both kingdoms—his general revelation to all people without distinction through *what he has made*, and his special revelation to his redeemed people through *what he has said*.

We find both forms of God's revelation in the first chapter of Genesis. The opening phrase of Scripture expresses the first form of God's revelation: "In the beginning God *created*." Creation itself is God's revelation—it is God revealing certain things to us, which is why we sometimes call this God's natural revelation or God's General revelation.

But then verse 3 of Genesis 1 expresses the second form of God's revelation: "And God *said*." And again in verses 6, 9, 11, 14, 20, 24, and 26 of Genesis 1, we find God revealing himself through spoken words. Then in verse 28 after he created Adam and Eve, "God blessed them. And God *said* to them." And then in Genesis 6:13, "God *said* to Noah." In Genesis 12, "the Lord *said* to Abram." In Exodus 3, God *called* to Moses out of the burning bush. Later at the foot of Mt. Sinai, God *spoke* the words of his law to his people. And as Hebrews 1 tells us, "long ago, at many times and in many ways, God *spoke* to our fathers by the prophets, but in these last days he has *spoken* to us by his Son."

In other words, God has revealed himself not only through what he has made, his natural revelation, but also through what he has said, what is sometimes referred to as God's special revelation. And many of these words were written down by holy men as they were carried along by the Holy Spirit (2 Pet 1:21), compiled into the Holy Scriptures, which Paul says "are able to make you wise for salvation through faith in Christ Jesus," these Scriptures being "breathed out by God" (2 Tim 3:15-16).

So God has revealed himself, and he has done so both through his natural revelation—what he has made—and through his special revelation—what he has said.

Perhaps one of the most succinct and, indeed, beautiful articulations of these two forms of God's revelation is found in Psalm 19. Verses 1-6 express God's natural revelation. "The heavens *declare* the glory of God, and the sky above *proclaims* his handiwork." This is the natural created order—heavens, skies, what God has made. And as these opening verses poignantly say, what God has made reveals certain things about him—creation is God's revelation. It reveals his glory and his handiwork. And not just some of creation, all of creation is God's revelation; the psalmist uses poetic expressions in verse 2 to communicate this: "Day to day pours out speech, and night to night reveals knowledge." From morning till evening, day and night, what God has made reveals his glory and handiwork; nature is God's speech and knowledge revealed to us. As Maltbie Babcock wrote, "This is my Father's world . . . in the rustling grass I hear him pass; he speaks to me everywhere" (1901).

But I want to stress one point here that we often take for granted because we say it so often: *Nature is God's revelation.* God created the heavens and the earth, and he did so intentionally to reveal himself. Nature is the voice of God. We know this, but I think sometimes, especially in our modern scientific, naturalistic society, we tend to view nature as apart from God, sort of doing its own thing. No, nature is God's revelation just like Scripture is, but it does differ from Scripture in a couple key ways, and they are communicated in Psalm 19.

First, *nature reveals God without words*. Notice what David says in verse 3: "There is no speech, nor are there words, whose voice is not heard." It's interesting—he just said in verse 2 that "day to day pours out speech," so nature is God's speech, but then he says just two phrases later, "there is no speech" in nature. In other words, David is clarifying what kind of revelation nature is. What God created is *like* speech—it reveals something about him, but it is not *exactly* speech. It is not actual words. We do not actually hear the audible voice of God in nature. When we sing, "in the rustling grass I hear him pass; he speaks to me everywhere," we don't mean that literally. There's no audible sound or voice.

But that does not make nature any less God's revelation. It just reveals God in ways other than words. God's spoken revelation does do some things that his natural revelation cannot, which we'll look at in a moment. But the fact that nature reveals God without words actually allows it to reveal God to us in ways that words cannot, which leads us to the next point:

God's natural revelation is universal. That cannot be said for his spoken special revelation—you have to be able to read, or at least listen to, Scripture in order to understand what God wants to reveal through Scripture. But what God reveals through what he has made is universal. This is what David communicates in verse 4: "Their voice goes out through all the earth, and their words to the end of the world." There is no place on earth, nor is there any person on earth where God's natural revelation does not reach—it is universal. In fact, the apostle Paul quotes this verse in Romans 10:18 to argue that Israel has no excuse for rejecting God's revelation, for "Their voice has gone out to all the earth, and their words to the ends of the world." God's natural revelation is universal. David uses the image of the sun to picture this:

> In them he has set a tent for the sun, [5] which comes out like a bridegroom leaving his chamber, and, like a strong man, runs its course with joy.

No one can escape the sun; it's universal.

> ⁶Its rising is from the end of the heavens, and its circuit to the end of them, and there is nothing hidden from its heat.

The same is true for God's natural revelation—nothing is hidden from it. Its voice goes out through all the earth, and its words to the end of the world. It is universal, which is why sometimes it is called "general revelation," meaning it reaches all people in general.

So what then is the nature of this universal, non-verbal revelation from God? Verse 3 says its voice is not heard, but verse 4 says its voice goes out through all the earth. So what is this voice?

Well, the Hebrew word in verse 4 literally means "line," which is often used of a measuring line, but that doesn't really make sense in this context. It can also be used for a line of text, like a line of poetry, which begins to fit a bit better.

But what's really interesting is how the Greek translators interpreted this word. I mentioned a moment ago that Paul quotes this verse in Romans 10:18, but of course, Paul is writing in Greek, so he's quoting the Greek translation of the Old Testament, the Septuagint. And the Septuagint uses a Greek word for "voice" that means "musical sound."

In other words, nature communicates revelation from God to us, not in actual words, but more like music—non-verbal communication of the beauty and order of God. Even ancient philosophers believed that music is the public demonstration of the harmony of heaven. They recognized an inherent order to the physical universe; they found that natural principles of physics, acoustics, geometry, and astronomy all share an amazing unity and that music was one of the best representations of that unity. They believed that music harmonized the universe; the intervals of music ordered all things, even the planets—they called it the "music of the spheres." They believed that the universe is characterized by a quality of interrelatedness that is highly evident in music.

And Christian theologians have long agreed with what those early philosophers recognized by God's common grace; they considered music to be a particularly powerful expression of the order and harmony of heaven. One of the earliest theologians of the church, Augustine, defined music as "the art of the well-ordered." God created the universe with an orderliness that displays his glory and handiwork universally to all people.

Natural revelation is the music of God, a display of his nature and the order of what he has made, and because it is not dependent upon words, natural revelation is universal. What music communicates is not limited to one group of people like spoken language is; music communicates at a natural level universally because it is part of God's created order, and this is what all nature does—it communicates naturally to all people regardless of language, ethnicity, or culture.

Paul highlights this universal power of general revelation in Romans 1 when he writes,

> For what can be known about God is plain to them, because God has shown it to them. [20] For his invisible attributes, namely, his eternal power and divine nature, have been clearly perceived, ever since the creation of the world, in the things that have been made. So they are without excuse.

So nature is God's revelation that universally communicates God's invisible attributes to all people, and because it does, Paul, says, *God's natural revelation condemns all people.* It is on the basis of natural revelation that Paul writes,

> For the wrath of God is revealed from heaven against all ungodliness and unrighteousness of men, who by their unrighteousness suppress the truth. (Rom 1:18)

We have no excuse, because God's general revelation is universal—it is all around us. In fact, God's natural revelation is within us. We are made in God's image, and so even our own existence reveals God to us. But as Paul says, even though God reveals himself to all people through what he has made, all people suppress the truth and are therefore deserving of God's wrath. God's natural revelation condemns all people.

This is the significance of understanding the reality of natural revelation for our discussion of the two kingdoms of God. God's natural revelation is universally available to all people. It is part of God's common grace to all people that he reveals transcendent, invisible attributes to them. It is on the basis of this universally communicated revelation that societies around the world throughout time have been able to survive; even without acknowledging God, unbelieving people made in God's image and living in his common kingdom nevertheless perceive universal principles upon which societies can survive to a certain degree.

However, the non-verbal, musical aspect of God's natural revelation that enables it to be universal is also a weakness—it cannot tell us specifics about the true God nor his Son, Jesus Christ. This is another reason it is called *general* revelation—it is general in that it is given to all mankind in general, and it is also general in that it only gives a general revelation of God. Natural revelation condemns all people, but it cannot reveal the remedy for that condemnation. This is why we need a second, special revelation from God.

Verse 7 of Psalm 19 shifts the focus from God's natural revelation to what some call his special revelation, specifically here "the law"—the Torah—"of the Lord." God's special revelation spoken of here by David is the 66 books of inscripturated Word of God. Paul calls God's special revelation "the sacred writings" and says that Scripture is "breathed out by God"—we use the term "inspired" to capture this truth (2 Tim 3:15-16). Human authors penned the words of Scripture, but Peter teaches that they "spoke from God as they were carried along by the Holy Spirit" (2 Pet 1:21). So the Bible is God's inspired special revelation.

God's inspired special revelation is sufficient to reveal God to us, just like his natural revelation does, but God's special revelation is also sufficient to transform us. That's what is communicated by the six benefits of God's law that David lists in the subsequent verses of Psalm 19: It revives the soul—complete transformation from death to life. Paul says the Word of God is "living and active, sharper than any two-edged sword, piercing to the division of soul and of spirit, of joints and of marrow, and discerning the thoughts and intentions of the heart" (Heb 4:12). And special revelation can do this, unlike natural revelation, because special revelation uses words. It tells us that we are guilty before God, and it tells us that whoever believes in the Lord Jesus Christ will be saved. God's special revelation uniquely reveals the gospel, which is the power of God for salvation to everyone who believes. And special revelation is profitable, as Paul says, to teach, reprove, correct, and train in righteousness, "that the man of God may be complete, equipped for every good work" (2 Tim 3:16-17).

David also says God's Word makes wise the simple. Wisdom is the ability to fit things together properly. We gather all the information of life around us, and wisdom enables us to know how to all fits together as God intended. My favorite illustration of the difference between knowledge and wisdom is that knowledge is knowing that a tomato is a fruit, but wisdom is knowing that a tomato doesn't belong in a fruit salad. The Bible makes us wise so that we are able to determine what kinds of things in this world *fit* with how God designed the world to work and with what he has revealed through both natural and special revelation.

In particular, Paul says that God's special revelation is able to make us "wise for salvation through faith in Christ Jesus." Natural revelation cannot do this, but God's Word, which reveals Jesus Christ to us, is able to recognize God's design for all creation to worship and glorify him, to recognize that sin destroys that purpose and deserves judgment, and that the only fitting response is unreserved faith in the sacrificial atonement of Jesus Christ, the Son of God.

But keep one very important truth in mind that distinguishes God's special revelation from his natural revelation: because it is expressed in written words, it is only sufficient for those who have those written words.

> How then will they call on him in whom they have not believed? And how are they to believe in him of whom they have never heard? And how are they to hear without someone preaching? (Rom 10:14)

Special revelation's strength is also a weakness—it is able to make us wise for salvation and transform us, but only if we read it. Natural revelation is more universal because it is non-verbal, but it can only condemn us; it cannot convert or transform us.

The importance for our discussion here is that transformation by and delight in God's special revelation is something important that distinguishes citizens of God's redemptive kingdom from those who are only citizens of God's common kingdom. We who are God's redeemed people have been regenerated by the Spirit through his Word. And thus we must live in light of, not only what God reveals through his natural revelation, but also what he reveals through his special revelation.

In all of how we live as citizens of the common kingdom of this world, we must never forget who we are—we are redeemed people with an inheritance preserved for us in heaven, and we must therefore faithfully submit ourselves to the special revelation that God has given to equip us for every good work in this present life. Scripture gives us everything we need to live God-pleasing lives as citizens of his common kingdom.

CHRISTIAN CITIZENS OF THE COMMON KINGDOM

In the next three chapters we are going to examine what it will look like for citizens of the redemptive kingdom to live in light of their true citizenship as model citizens of the common kingdom. We will discuss what the Bible teaches about how we should view our vocations, families, government, and culture making.

However, before we get into specifics, I want to lay a foundation by focusing on the general principles that Scripture says ought to characterize Christian citizens of the common kingdom.

For example, in 1 Peter 3:8 and following, Peter urges redeemed citizens to strive to be the kind of people who dwell in unity, sympathy, brotherly love, tenderness of heart, and humility. As Paul says in Romans 12, we ought to strive to live peaceably with all. He says in 1 Timothy 2 that our goal in society should be to "lead a peaceful and quiet life, godly and dignified in every way." If we do that, if we live as good, faithful citizens, then chances are we're going to have a positive impact on society at large because we are living in the common kingdom as God intended when he instituted it in the garden.

That ought to be our goal as citizens of the common kingdom, but because of sin, and because we are distinct from the other citizens—because we are ultimately exiles—we should not expect to be entirely comfortable. "All who desire to live a godly life in Christ Jesus will be persecuted" (2 Tim 3:12). That is really the context for Peter's letter. The Christians to whom he was writing were beginning to experience persecution, and so he urges them to live godly lives, live in harmony with all, and keep their conduct among the Gentiles honorable, so that "when you are slandered, those who revile your good behavior in Christ may be put to shame" (1 Pet 3:16). Live for the good of all people in society, expect the possibility of persecution for your faith, and don't give them any legitimate reason to condemn you.

Look at how Peter further describes our lives as Christians in the world in chapter 4:

> The end of all things is at hand; therefore be self-controlled and sober-minded for the sake of your prayers. ⁸ Above all, keep loving one another earnestly, since love covers a multitude of sins. ⁹ Show hospitality to one another without grumbling. ¹⁰ As each has received a gift, use it to serve one another, as good stewards of God's varied grace: ¹¹ whoever speaks, as one who speaks oracles of God; whoever serves, as one who serves by the strength that God supplies—in order that in everything God may be glorified through Jesus Christ. To him belong glory and dominion forever and ever. Amen. (4:7-11)

We must live with our eyes on the end of all thing. Everything about how we Christians live in society should be uniquely characterized by our Christian beliefs and values: self-control, sobriety, love, hospitality, and service, ultimately all for God's glory.

And notice how Peter ends his letter:

> Be sober-minded; be watchful. Your adversary the devil prowls around like a roaring lion, seeking someone to devour. ⁹ Resist him, firm in your faith, knowing that the same kinds of suffering are being experienced by your brotherhood throughout the world. ¹⁰ And after you have suffered a little while, the God of all grace, who has called you to his eternal glory in Christ, will himself restore, confirm, strengthen, and establish you. ¹¹ To him be the dominion forever and ever. Amen. (5:8–11)

Ultimately, our hope is not in this present world. Our blessed hope is the appearing of the glory of our great God and Savior Jesus Christ. To *him* be the dominion forever and ever. Amen.

4

CHRISTIAN FAITHFULNESS

What does it really mean to serve the Lord? Have you ever thought about that?

Unfortunately, there is actually a lot of confusion about the proper answer to that question among evangelicals today. Some Christians believe that the only way to really serve the purposes and plans of God is what is sometimes referred to as "full-time Christian service." All other vocations are just "secular" and therefore are of lesser value. If you're a farmer or a firefighter or a contractor or a computer programmer, those jobs are not really service to the Lord. If you really want to serve Christ, then you should pursue being a pastor or missionary. And women—well, you're out of luck. You can't really serve Christ full-time because you can't be a pastor, and you're stuck at home with the kids.

The New Testament completely corrects this way of thinking. For example, at the end of his letter to the Colossian church, Paul gives some instructions for people in various stations of life. He addresses wives, husbands, children, fathers—and by implication parents in general, bondservants, and finally masters—everyday, normal life functions that people have in the world. "Secular" work.

But as we saw in the last chapter, Paul isn't discussing these topics randomly; he does so in the context of instructing how citizens of the redemptive kingdom should live in everyday situations that are common even to unbelieving people. As Peter does, so Paul wants Christians to live in these common situations in a distinct way because of our redemption.

Just before Paul gives instructions regarding these common situations, he writes,

> And whatever you do, in word or deed, do everything in the name of the Lord Jesus, giving thanks to God the Father through him. (Col 3:17)

Paul has just spent some time in Colossians helping us understand what it means to serve the Lord. "Set your minds on things that are above, not on things that are on earth," he said in 3:2. "Put to death what is earthly in you" (v. 5); put on spiritual affections, let the peace of Christ rule in your hearts, let the word of Christ dwell in you richly . . . in other words, verse 17, "whatever you do, in word or deed, do everything in the name of the Lord Jesus, giving thanks to God the Father through him.

But then comes the real life, rubber-meets-the-road question: *Here I am, I'm a shoemaker in the local village; I work hard to put food on the table, I get up early, work hard all day, get home exhausted, and get up the next day and do it* all over again; how, really, can I obey what Paul just commanded in the first half of chapter 3? I mean, Paul said to set my affections on things above, not on things that are on earth, but I have all these earthly concerns to deal with.

What does it really mean to set my affections on things above? What does it mean to do everything in the name of the Lord Jesus? In order to do that, do I need to give up my job as a shoemaker and go be a pastor? Or maybe, if I just print Scripture verses on all the shoes I make, why then I can service Christ in my vocation, right? What does that really look like practically? Can I really serve Christ in all of those spiritual ways when I'm so busy and distracted with all this necessary but seemingly earthly, non-spiritual, day-to-day labor?

Or, maybe there's a housewife sitting there listening to this letter being read on a Lord's Day morning and she thinks, *I really want to serve Christ this way, but I have to get up early every morning and go down to the market to buy the food for the day, and I've got three little kids hanging on my legs, and I spend most of the day just baking bread and preparing food and scrubbing floors and wiping runny noses—how can I find time to serve the Lord in the midst of all of that?*

And you have the same with business owners in the congregation, and teachers, lawyers, doctors, children, sailors, soldiers—they're all sitting there thinking the same thing: *I really want to serve Christ, but I'm so busy with other things that need to get done. I mean, I can see how Pastor Epaphras can serve the Lord—he gets to do truly spiritual things all day, every day. He gets to study the Bible and pray* for much longer periods of time than I ever have time for, he counsels people's spiritual needs, he does the work of the ministry of the church; I have a real job; I have duties at home. How in the world can I find time to serve Christ?

Paul anticipates this concern and addresses it head on. He speaks to various kinds of people like wives, husbands, children, parents, bondservants, and masters—people with real life concerns and duties and responsibilities and burdens, and he talks to them about how they can serve Christ, not *apart* from their everyday duties and responsibilities, but how they can serve Christ *within* their everyday work.

You see, when Paul says in verse 24, "You are serving the Lord Christ," Paul is talking about every single one of the vocations mentioned in the context. Wives, he says, when you do what wives are designed by God to do, which includes the everyday responsibilities of a wife, you are serving the Lord Christ. Husbands, he says, when you do your job as a husband, you are serving the Lord Christ. Then he moves to children and parents. When you do your job as a child or as a parent, you are serving the Lord Christ.

And then, perhaps most remarkable of all, we get to Colossians 3:22 where Paul addresses *bondservants*. Now perhaps we can see how wives and husbands and children and parents are all God-ordained vocations in which we can legitimately serve him; but servants? We can see how God created husbands and wives and parents and children, but bondservant is a station in life that people created. Surely that's got to be one of the most secular of all jobs.

In fact, when you read "servants" in Colossians 3, don't think someone who flips burgers at McDonalds or who works the checkout at Walmart or a butler in a mansion. A bondservant in the time Paul wrote was one of the absolute worst, bottom-of-the-barrel stations of life in which someone could find himself. Bondservants usually owed some kind of debt to their masters, had to do the dirtiest most menial kinds of work, and were often paid very poorly.

And yet, Paul looks at these individuals whose jobs include some of the most mundane, earthly, secular work, and he says to them, in your job as a bondservant, you are serving the Lord Christ. What a remarkable thought. Paul is intentionally choosing the lowliest of all professions and calling it service to Christ as a way of saying all legitimate human vocations in life are service to the Lord Christ. There is no legitimate profession that is somehow inferior in its ability to serve Christ than another. There are, perhaps, some *illegitimate* professions, but you can serve the Lord Christ in all legitimate professions.

In other words, being a pastor or a missionary are services to Christ, but they are not more spiritual than being an accountant, a printer, an electrician, a computer programmer, or a stay-at-home mom. All legitimate vocations can be full-time Christian service. And not just in that you can make money to use for ministry, or you can perhaps find opportunities to witness for Christ in your job, though those are both wonderful to do.

No, you can actually serve the Lord Christ *in* punching keys on a keyboard, balancing accounts, building houses, fixing leaks, and wiping noses.

COMMON GRACE INSTITUTIONS

So why is this the case? Why is it that we as Christians can serve Christ just as significantly in what we might consider "secular" work as a pastor can?

It is because, as we have seen, God is at work in this world in two significant ways. On the one hand, he absolutely is working to build his redemptive kingdom. Christ said, "I will build my church." He's doing that. And he's doing that through us, his people, when we share the gospel, when we build up and encourage one another in the faith, when pastors preach and disciple believers, when we gather for corporate worship. In each of these activities, we are serving as ministers of God as he works to superintend over his redemptive kingdom.

But that is not all God is doing in the world. God is also working in this world to superintend his universal common kingdom. He is sovereignly working to preserve order and peace in a sinful world. And just like in the redemptive kingdom he uses people as tools to do that work, so in the common kingdom God uses people to accomplish his work in various realms. Some of how God rules in these two ways is indirectly through providence. He might use weather, for example, to orchestrate his will among the peoples of the earth.

However, God has also chosen to exercise his rule in both respects through human beings. In terms of his redemptive rule over his chosen people, God rules in this age through his church by the authority of Scripture and the mandate Christ gave her—make disciples (Matt 28:19). We will focus on this in chapter 7.

On the other hand, God has chosen to exercise his universal rule over all things partly through common grace human institutions that he created to maintain order and flourishing in the world, including family, human vocations, and government.

FAMILY

In Genesis 2:18-24, God established the institution of marriage—and by extension, family—as one of the fundamental building blocks of human society and one of the central human institutions he would use to cultivate and preserve order and flourishing in his world.

However, though the underlying purpose for the family is part of God's created order for all people for their good, God's redeemed people nevertheless function in family life uniquely because of their distinct beliefs and values. And so the New Testament helps Christians understand how they ought to function in this God-ordained common grace institution.

For example, both Paul and Peter addresses the human institution of the family, articulating principles that apply to all families but that will find unique significance for Christians (Eph 5:22-6:4; Col 3:18-21; 1 Pet 3:1-7). Wives are to be subject to their husbands. This is not because women are somehow inferior to men; rather, for the ordering of society, even before the fall, God established at creation a certain order: he made Adam first, and then he made Eve out of Adam as a helper fit for him. On the basis of this creation norm, Paul says in 1 Corinthians 11 that the head of a wife is her husband, and thus wives ought to submit to their husbands, which is a voluntary ordering of herself under his leadership. So again, the purpose of this command is for the good of society within the common kingdom.

Peter commands husbands, likewise, to live with their wives in an understanding way (1 Pet 3:7), and in Ephesians 5:25 Paul says husbands ought to love their wives as Christ loves the church. This is a sort of submission, too, not a submission to the wife as a leader, but leading through a loving submission to her needs. A husband should arrange his own desires and needs under the needs of his wife as a weaker vessel. Again, a wife is not inferior to her husband; as Peter says next, Christian wives are fellow heirs with their husbands—they are equal citizens in the redemptive kingdom. But God created Eve out of Adam, and thus husbands are responsible to lovingly lead their wives, submitting their desires to the needs of their wives. The world sees this arrangement as oppressive, but God meant it for our good.

Further, children are to obey their parents, and Christian fathers are specifically commanded to bring up their children "in the discipline and instruction of the Lord" (Eph 6:4). As was true of the redeemed Israelites (Deut 6:6–9), Christian parents are to fervently pass on to their children the central essence of what it means to be a citizen of the redemptive kingdom, including right beliefs about God, an all-encompassing love for him, and a life of obedience to his commands. Christian parents ought to rear children to know God, love God, and obey God, and this requires making these emphases a pervasive part of everyday life.

The point here is that family matters. For the glory of God, the salvation and sanctification of our own children and others around us, and for the benefit of society in general, it matters how we discipline and educate our children. Don't underestimate the deep importance of cultivating strong marriages and rearing godly children. As sojourners and exiles, we ought to do all of these things in light of the fact that we are people of God. God requires Christian faithfulness in family matters for his glory and our own good.

GOD'S MASKS

Likewise, God also has ordained ordinary, everyday human work as a means by which he providentially rules his common kingdom. This is why it is important to recognize the value of human work as service for God that requires Christian faithfulness.

A kind of thinking that says only full-time church workers are really doing ministry actually perpetuated during the Middle Ages. The medieval Church taught that being a pastor was really the only calling of God; all other professions were simply necessary evils. And so it is in the seventeenth-century Reformers that we get some of the most helpful biblical arguments against this perspective.

Martin Luther was particularly brilliant in combatting this way of thinking and in arguing that God works through every legitimate profession. He used Psalm 147:13, for example, to explain the biblical perspective. The verse reads, "For God strengthens the bars of your gates;" How does God strengthen the bars, Luther asks? By city planners and architects; by politicians who pass good laws to protect the city. The psalm continues, "God blesses your children within you." How does he bless our children, Luther asks? Through the work of teachers and pediatricians. The psalm continues, "God makes peace in your borders." How? By means of good lawyers and policemen. "God fills you with the finest of the wheat." How? By farmers, factory workers, bakers, and grocers.

Luther went on to say this: "When we pray the Lord's Prayer, we ask God to 'give us this day our daily bread.' And he does give us our daily bread. He does it by means of the farmer who planted and harvested the grain, the baker who made the flour into bread, the person who prepared our meal." God answers our prayer for daily bread through each of these vocations. Our legitimate professions, Luther said, are like the "masks" God wears in caring for the world. They are God's work!

When you teach something that is true to a student and help to make her better for it, you are doing God's work. When you fix someone's computer problem so that he can do their job better, you are doing God's work. When you sell someone a product that will enrich his life, you are doing God's work. When you vacuum under the kitchen table for the zillionth time to keep your home clean and healthy, you are doing God's work.

Now don't get me wrong; preaching, sharing the gospel with someone, teaching in a Bible study, and going on mission trips are indeed service to the Lord within his redemptive kingdom. And being a pastor or a missionary are wonderful, God-ordained ministries, but *only if* that is what God has called you to do. You can and you should serve the Lord Christ in whatever God has called you to be.

If God has called you to be an electrician, and instead you pursue being a pastor, then that is the worst thing you could do. If God has called you to be a computer programmer, and instead you pursue being a missionary, then you are out of God's will for you. If God has called you to be an electrician or a computer programmer, you can serve the Lord Christ in those callings.

CALLING

Often in Christian circles when we talk about a "calling," we tend to use that term only to describe being called as a pastor or missionary. But again, limiting calling to only ministry positions within the church is not what Scripture teaches.

The best text that helps us see this is in 1 Corinthians 7. Notice what Paul says in verse 17:

> Only let each person lead the life that the Lord has assigned to him, and to which God has called him. This is my rule in all the churches. (1 Cor 7:17)

Here Paul is discussing God's calling on your life, but notice that nowhere in this context is he specifically talking about calling to ministry in the church. Rather, he is in the midst of a discussion of various regular life situations in which Christians may find themselves. He just finished talking about a Christian wife who is married to an unbelieving husband. He's going to move on to discuss those who are circumcised or uncircumcised, people who are bondservants, people who are betrothed, people who are unmarried, people who are married—all sorts of various life situations.

And what does Paul say in verse 17 about every one of these situations? This is what the Lord has assigned you. If you are single, a wife or a husband, if you have children or don't have children, if you are a manager or a bottom-rung paper pusher, rich or poor, living in a wonderful Christian marriage or struggling with an unbelieving spouse, this is the life to which God has *called* you. This is your calling from the Lord, no different from a calling to be a pastor; this is your vocation, which just comes from the Latin word for calling. And that is why, no matter what your calling, from the pastor of a prominent megachurch to a woman who sells crafts on Etsy, you can serve the Lord Christ in your calling.

Now, sometimes we know the life God has assigned for us simply because that's where we find ourselves with really very little intentional decision on our part; that's what Paul is mostly addressing in 1 Corinthians 7. A woman is married, she comes to faith in Christ, and now here she is married to an unsaved man; what should she do? She should see that as the Lord's calling in her life, and she should serve the Lord Christ in that. Or here is a man, and through no fault of his own, the economy turns bad, he loses a bunch of investments, and he finds himself indebted as a bondservant; what should he do? He should see that as the Lord's calling in his life, and he should serve the Lord Christ in that.

But often, especially in our prosperous day and age, we actually have a lot of choice regarding what we're going to do with our lives. Many times things happen that we don't control, but many times we can actually pursue a vocation. So how do you know what God has called you to do? Sometimes there is lack of clarity on this point, again, because of a sort of mystical view of calling that developed erroneously during the Middle Ages.

God is not going to call you to a particular profession by whispering in your ear one night; he's not going to call you by writing a message in the clouds or through a dream by giving you some sort of mystical feeling in your bosom. If you're waiting for some kind of feeling or audible message to know God's call for your life, you're either going to be mistaken or you'll be waiting a long time. God has made clear that we have a more sure Word of prophecy today (2 Pet 1:19), we have the Word of God which is sufficient to equip us to every good work (2 Tim 3:17). And through the wisdom that comes only from faithfully reading and meditating on God's Word, God directs us into the vocations that he has for us.

God uses abilities and desires that he has given you to direct you, he orchestrates circumstances and opportunities for you in the course of your life, and he uses wise counsel and confirmation from others in your life to guide you into the particular assignment he has for your life. We need to use wisdom that comes from him in his Word to assess how he is working and what he is doing through the circumstances of life and then work to serve him in whatever calling he has placed us.

But the bottom line is that if God has called you to do something through equipping you, through giving you opportunities, and through affirmation by others, or just through circumstances out of your control, then that is the most important, high calling for you. Nothing else is a higher calling for you. And in that calling, you can serve the Lord Christ in just as significant a spiritual way as a pastor or a missionary can. You can serve the Lord Christ through being a student; you can serve the Lord Christ through being a teacher. You can serve the Lord Christ as a bus driver, a banker, a mayor, a judge, a janitor, or as a stay-at-home mother.

HOW TO SERVE CHRIST IN YOUR WORK

So how, then, can we serve the Lord Christ in all of these callings? What Paul says to bondservants in verse 22 of Colossians 3 can equally apply to you no matter what vocation you are in.

First, Paul says, "obey in everything those who are your earthly masters." In other words, fulfill the responsibilities given to you in whatever calling you find yourself. Sometimes those responsibilities are clearly defined and given to you by an earthly master, other times you have a more general picture of what needs to get done and it's up to you to define the specific duties. Either way, when you simply do your job, you are serving the Lord Christ.

And even if you're the one defining the responsibilities—you're the boss, you're the manager, you're the head of the household—even then, don't forget as Paul says in Colossians 4:1, "you also have a Master in heaven." I regularly tell my kids that they need to learn now how to submit to their authorities when they're young, and when their authorities love them and want their best, because there will never be a day when they don't have someone telling them what to do; and someday, those telling them what to do might not necessarily have their best interest in mind.

But if Paul can tell bondservants to serve the Lord Christ *through* obeying their masters, then surely it is true for us that we should serve the Lord Christ even when working under an unreasonable or unfair boss. And when we do our job, when we submit to our authorities, when we fulfill the responsibilities required of us, even if they seem mundane and the very antithesis of spiritual, we are serving the Lord Christ.

But the motivation for fulfilling your responsibilities also matters: don't do your job by way of eye-service, as people-pleasers, Paul says in Colossian 4:22. If that's why you're doing what you're supposed to do, then you aren't serving the Lord Christ, you are serving yourself. No, do your job with sincerity of heart. Do it because it's right.

Do it out of a desire to serve others. Do your job, whatever that might be, ultimately out of fear of the Lord. And if you're working for the Lord and not ultimately for people, then you're not just going to do the minimum to fulfill your requirements, you're going to go above and beyond to do the best job possible.

And that leads to the next point Paul makes in verse 23: "Whatever you do, work heartily"—not half-heartedly, not just doing the minimum; work *heartily*. Why? Because you're doing it for the Lord and not for men. You're not fixing that computer problem just to please the customer or so that your boss doesn't get a bad report about you, you're doing it for the Lord, so do it heartily. You're selling products, not so you get a nice bonus at the end of the year; you're doing it for the Lord, so do it heartily. Students, you're reading those books, memorizing those facts, and studying for those tests not just to get a good grade and a good GPA and recognition; you're doing it for the Lord, so do it heartily. Mom, you're wiping those noses, washing those clothes, and making those meals, not to get accolades from others; you're doing it for the Lord, so do it heartily. Christian bakers should bake the best bread possible. Christian bankers should invest their clients' money with the highest integrity. Christian auto mechanics should fix cars to the best of their abilities, because they are doing it for the Lord.

Because ultimately, if you are doing what you do for human approval or accolades or rewards, remember what Jesus said? He said, if you practice righteousness before other people in order to be seen by them, then you've received all the reward you'll ever get—you will have no reward from your Father who is in heaven (Matt 6:1-2).

Peter addresses the subject of human vocation as well in 1 Peter 3:18-25. He teaches we ought to submit to our authorities in our human vocations:

> Servants, be subject to your masters with all respect, not only to the good and gentle but also to the unjust. [19] For this is a gracious thing, when, mindful of God, one endures sorrows while suffering unjustly. (1 Pet 2:18-19)

Here Peter addresses the servant/master relationship, which is obviously the most extreme kind of employee/employer relationship. But in a sense, that makes his point even stronger. If Peter tells a servant to be subject to his master, how much more ought we who simply have a supervisor or manager over us submit to them? Arguing from greater to lesser, Peter's primary point here is simply that in our human vocation, we ought to submit to our authorities, whatever form that might take.

And notice that Peter further addresses what might be extreme examples to make his point. We are to submit to employers, not just when they are good and gentle, but also when they are unjust. When we are treated unjustly, we do not have the right, Peter says, to rise up and rebel. Even oppressed slaves were to endure suffering without responding wrongly. Again, arguing from worse to better, how much more ought we to submit when we simply get overlooked for a promotion, or are given a larger workload than another employee, or mistreated in some other way? And if it happens that we are mistreated, especially if we are mistreated *because* we are Christians, Peter says that this is actually a gracious thing since it reflects Christ's own suffering. We ought to follow his example: when he suffered, he did not sin in response.

In whatever we do in our earthly vocations, we need to always remember, as Paul reminds us in Colossian 3:24, that it is from the Lord that we will receive the inheritance as our reward. The word "receive" there has the idea of receiving what is due and receiving it in full. This can be great comfort and encouragement to us in our vocations. You might work hard and go above and beyond your official job description, and yet from an earthly perspective you still get overlooked for the promotion and never get noticed and never get the bonus, and even get complaints and criticized unjustly. But you're not doing it for them! You are serving the Lord Christ! And one day he will give you your fitting and full reward, a place of honor in his sight.

The central point is this: pastors, missionaries, Bible study teachers, and church organists serve the Lord Christ in various ministries within the church. But you can serve the Lord Christ with just as much value and spiritual significance and heavenly reward as a printer, doctor, electrician, accountant, or housewife.

5

GOD'S SERVANTS FOR OUR GOOD

God is Sovereign King, and he takes care of his world. In his common grace, he even takes care of those who reject him, and as we have seen, he does so through particular common grace institutions that he created. These include the institution of family, common human vocations, and as we will address in this chapter, human government.

GOD'S SERVANTS

In Genesis 9:6—notably *after* the Fall and *after* the Flood—God established the institution of human government:

> Whoever sheds the blood of man, by man shall his blood be shed, for God made man in his own image.

God gave the responsibility of capital punishment—an exercise of *his* just judgment of sin—to all humankind as a means through which he would sovereignly control man's sinfulness and preserve the world and its order.

This responsibility, which takes shape in formal human governments over the course of history, has been given to humankind collectively, not just believing people. Thus, even unbelieving governors, when they exercise justice against wrongdoing, are an extension of God's universal rule.

Romans 13:1 emphasizes this point:

> Let every person be subject to the governing authorities. For there is no authority except from God, and those that exist have been instituted by God.

The governing authority Paul references is not the redemptive rule of God over his people; this is the earthly administration of making and enforcing laws that preserve peace and justice in the common, everyday affairs of life. This kind of earthly rule—a rule that comes with authority derived from the ultimate Ruler—has been instituted by God himself. Even something seemingly mundane and "earthly" has been instituted by God in just the same way as he instituted the church and rulers within the government of God's redeemed people.

What is remarkable about this passage is the Roman political situation in which Paul wrote this. For over 500 years Rome had existed as a republic, but it was now transitioning to a monarchy. Emperor Nero had gained power after his mother had poisoned his father, and under Nero's reign persecution against the Jews and Christians was on the rise and taxes were oppressive. It is in this less-than-ideal political situation that Paul instructs Christians to "be subject to governing authorities."

Why? Because "there is no authority except from God, and those that exist have been instituted by God." As we have seen, God instituted human government, however imperfect, as a common grace institution with the purpose of maintaining peace and order in a sin-cursed world.

And not only that, look at what Paul says about a governmental ruler who does what God has instituted in punishing wrongdoing and protecting the innocent:

> ... for he is God's servant for your good. But if you do wrong, be afraid, for he does not bear the sword in vain. For he is the servant of God, an avenger who carries out God's wrath on the wrongdoer. (Rom 13:4)

Do you see what he is saying there? A government employee like a governor, legislator, judge, or police officer who does his job and enforces laws that help to establish peace and order in society *is a servant of God*. And what does Paul say at the end of the verse? When he punishes wrongdoing, he is actually carrying out *God's* wrath on the wrongdoer. Paul calls magistrates literally "deacons of God," but he says this of pagan Roman governors who didn't even acknowledge the fact; indeed, they did not believe it. But nevertheless, they *were* deacons of God when they carried out God's wrath, similar to how the Lord called King Cyrus his "anointed" (Is 45:1). God is ruling over his universal, common kingdom, and he is doing that *through* unbelieving human rulers.

However, the other important point to recognize here is that since God is the one who instituted human government as an extension of his providential rule over all, *human governments are subject to the moral law of God*. Human governments are not ultimate; governments must operate as God intended them to operate.

And indeed, even pagan rulers can abide by and enforce the moral law of God. Paul articulates in Romans 2:14-15 the reality of "when Gentiles, who do not have the law, by nature do what the law requires . . . even though they do not have the law. They show that the work of the law is written on their hearts, while their conscience also bears witness, and their conflicting thoughts accuse or even excuse them." This is what Greg Bahnsen referred to as "borrowed capital"—pagans borrowing biblical values in certain areas of their lives.[1] Even though it is inconsistent with what they say they believe, pagans made in God's image nevertheless sometimes take advantage of his common grace and do what the law requires.

This does not mean that the realm of politics is somehow a "neutral sphere." The fact is that there is no

---

[1] Greg L. Bahnsen, *Pushing the Antithesis: The Apologetic Methodology of Greg L. Bahnsen* (Powder Springs, GA: American Vision, 2007), 103.

neutrality on any issue; every matter is either consistent with God's law or it contradicts God's law. There is only right or wrong, good or bad, light or dark. The only grounding for successful living that makes consistent sense in God's world is one rooted in the authoritative truth of God's holy Word and repentant faith in Christ.

Yet because all men are made in the image of God (Gen 1:27), because "the heavens are telling the glory of God" (Ps 19:1) and God's "invisible attributes, namely, his eternal power and divine nature, have been clearly perceived, ever since the creation of the world, in the things that have been made" (Rom 1:20), and because God shows common grace even to the unjust (Matt 5:45), unbelieving people often reflect a transcendent morality in their lives that in actuality is inconsistent with their stated belief system.

COMMON GRACE POLITICS

So governments that help to establish and enforce general morality in society are doing God's work to preserve peace and order even when those governments do not even acknowledge or recognize that they are doing so. And the fact is, all successful political systems throughout world history have done this to one degree or another. Societies with pagan magistrates throughout history have sought to build their political systems on transcendent morality, even though they could not fully account for that morality. The pagan Greco/Roman thought of Paul's day embodied transcendent moral grounding for its political philosophy as they applied God's law written on their hearts.

C. S. Lewis makes this observation in both *Mere Christianity* and *The Abolition of Man*, and in the latter he provides an appendix of many examples of civic laws from various nations around the world that are an embodiment of transcendent morality that ultimately comes from God. These are the very laws that we ought to be promoting and supporting in our own legal system. Pagans can recognize the wisdom of these laws and keep them, though in truth, to do so is inconsistent with their own pagan worldview.

Throughout history, pagans have often figured out successful legal systems that reflect biblical values because, since God designed the world to work in a certain way, those kinds of systems just work best for the order and prosperity of a society. That's the reality of common grace politics. The truth is that in matters of the state, the only two options are not Christ or chaos. In his kind providence, God specifically designed human government to provide a third common grace option given to all humankind (not just his redeemed people) that imperfectly preserves a degree of order and peace until Christ establishes his perfect theocratic Kingdom on earth.

God's covenant with Noah in Genesis 9 reveals God's plan to preserve humankind and creation until the

Second Adam establishes his earthly rule. Because of the reality of human rebellion, God provided measures by which in his providence he would preserve the stability of a cursed world through the earthly institution of human government, with its God-given responsibility of capital punishment. Before the Flood, it was Christ or chaos, and it quickly devolved into chaos. After Genesis 9, and especially after Babel, nations formed and prevented chaos as God works his plan of redemption for his people.

Now, it is important to recognize that no human government is perfect; none will be until Jesus comes again. But imperfect, common grace order is why God created human government, not utopia. Utopia will come when the King comes.

LIMITED GOVERNMENT

It is also important, however, to recognize that since God is the one who instituted government, government has limited jurisdiction. God's initial institution of government in Genesis 9 explicitly designated the specific jurisdiction God appointed for the institution: the protection of human life. Additionally, Romans 13 also reiterates the kind of morality government has been charged with enforcing:

> Owe no one anything, except to love each other, for the one who loves another has fulfilled the law. [9] For

the commandments, "You shall not commit adultery, You shall not murder, You shall not steal, You shall not covet," and any other commandment, are summed up in this word: "You shall love your neighbor as yourself." [10] Love does no wrong to a neighbor; therefore love is the fulfilling of the law. (Rom 13:8-10)

In other words, the context of Paul's discussion of governing authorities indicates what aspects of God's moral law God has appointed government to enforce, namely, what we call the "Second Table" of God's law (Commandments six through ten). These are God's moral laws that involve human relationships.

Note that government has not been given jurisdiction to enforce *all* of God's moral law. Magistrates have not been tasked with enforcing the First Table of God's moral law, those laws involving human relationship to God. Adherence to those laws comes only when the Holy Spirit of God regenerates a human heart, writing those laws upon the heart so that believers in Jesus Christ voluntarily submit themselves to those laws. Thus, establishment of the First Table of God's moral law falls under the jurisdiction of the church, not government, and only through divine weapons of the Word (more on this later).

So this means extremely limited government that has jurisdiction exclusively involving the punishment of murder, theft, and other crimes against human life and safety. As Thomas Jefferson famously quipped, "government is best which governs least." Full theocracy is not the goal, but simply the preservation of human life and safety in a sin-cursed world.

THE DANGERS OF GOVERNMENT-ENFORCED RELIGION

Some Christians today, however, argue that government ought to enforce *both* Tables of the Law and ought to move toward the establishment of "Christian nations" or "Christendom." However, as we have already seen, human government has been given a specific, limited jurisdiction. Furthermore, Christendom has been tried before, and it failed each time it was tried since obedience to God's moral law only comes ultimately when individuals submit themselves to him in repentant faith.

THE THEOCRACY OF ISRAEL

The first time "Christendom" was tried was explicitly instituted by God himself in the nation of Israel. I use "Christendom" here, of course, anachronistically, but the reality is that Israel was a theocracy, meaning that there was no "separation of church and state"; rather, religious life and civil life were intertwined. As we have seen, God established this holy theocracy as a picture of his intended goal for the whole world. All members of the nation were considered the people of God and expected to live in conformity to the Law of God, though certainly not every individual in the nation was a "true Israelite"; that is, many (most?) in the nation did not have personal faith in God.

MEDIEVAL CHRISTENDOM

The multi-ethnic nature of the New Testament church changed this reality as Christianity spread outside Israel to other nations, and especially once Israel as a nation fell in AD 70. However, church/state union was formed once again after Roman Emperor Constantine I legalized Christianity in 313 with the Edict of Milan, and especially when Emperor Theodosius I made Christianity the Roman Empire's official religion in 391 and in the following year outlawed any form of pagan worship. This began a period that has come explicitly to be called "Christendom."

In medieval Christendom, the church began to be the controlling influence in the entirety of the Roman empire. This shifted what had once been a severely persecuted church to the center of western society, eventually leading to what many believed to be a "Christian civilization"—a "Holy Roman Empire." Later, Holy Roman Emperor Charlemagne forced thousands of Saxons to be baptized at the point of a sword. This achieved lots of baptisms, but no true conversions.

The Protestant Reformation fragmented "The Church," which ended unified Christian dominance over society, and the rapid rise of secularism during the Enlightenment put the nail in Christendom's coffin. However, in the wake of the Protestant Reformation, many European countries continued very close relationships between the state and state-sponsored churches, prime examples being the prominence of Lutheranism in Germany, the Anglican Church in England, and the Dutch Reformed Church in the Netherlands.

Furthermore, the effects of Christendom lingered for centuries throughout Europe, perhaps climaxing in the founding of the United States of America. We are still experiencing some of the positive benefits of Christendom in the United States today.

BENEFITS OF CHRISTENDOM

Were there benefits that came from these "Christian nations"? Certainly. Let's notice just three prime examples.

The first is the most obvious and really the greatest benefit: the formation of Christendom freed Christians to worship according to their consciences. As mentioned above, prior to the Edict of Milan in 313, Christians were forced to gather in secret, often fearful of imprisonment or death.

Second, Christendom no doubt allowed morality to flourish in society. When there is a union of church and state, biblical norms come to carry the most significant influence upon the laws of the land and even the moral expectations of culture. Few would question the benefits of what some call a "Judeo-Christian ethic" upon the development of laws in the early years of the United States, for example.

This is a blessing in a society, because things just work better when the standards of a society are based upon how God designed the world to work. A society in which marriages and families are strong, general moral standards are high, and sin is frowned upon and even punished in the public sphere is going to be a society that flourishes and prospers.

A third benefit of Christendom has been stunningly beautiful cultural production rooted in the transcendent beauty and order of God himself. This is undoubtedly true: Rembrandt, da Vinci, and Bach were possible only because of Christendom. The kinds of complex, beautiful works of art created by men like these presupposed an orderliness and transcendence found uniquely in biblical Christianity. The fact that other cultures have not produced that level of art has nothing to do with ethnicity and everything to do with the biblical values that lay at the core of western Christendom.

Not only art, but also advancements in science, politics, economics, industry, and technology occurred uniquely in the West due to the dominance of Christian values. Wonder in God's world and genuine desire to improve conditions for fellow humankind flow from Christianity and impact the world in positive ways.

THE HARM OF CHRISTENDOM

There is no doubt in my mind whatsoever that if a nation were Christian—that is, if Christianity were the official religion of a nation such that laws and culture were strongly dominated by biblical values, that nation would be better off in terms of public morality and cultural production.

However, these very external blessings possess a devastating effect: Christendom creates a cultural Christianity that actually hinders the church's mission of making disciples.

Since in a Christian nation the very fabric of society is considered "Christian," citizens of such a nation do not recognize their inherent depravity and need to repent of their sin and put their unreserved faith in Christ alone for their salvation. In the consciousness of such citizens, they are "Christian" by virtue of their citizenship; there is no "opt in" to Christianity in Christendom—citizens have already been "baptized" into the Christian community.

Consider the "Bible belt" in the southern United States, for example. How many people fail to put their trust in Christ because they do not even recognize their need of salvation due to the fact that a form of cultural

Christianity still dominates in much of the South? How many Evangelical mega-churches are filled with nominal, "cultural Christians"? Even the theocracy of Israel proved that a national religion that forced people into conformity with God's Law was not enough to bring people into a true personal relationship with God. A new covenant was needed in which the very hearts of individuals were transformed by the Spirit of God. Inner regeneration must precede external conformity to God's Law.

Likewise, contrary to what some might claim, cultural Christianity does not lead people toward Christ, it actually desensitizes them to true Christianity and eventually leads to apathy and agnosticism. For example, one core cause of the prevalent secularism of Europe and the United Kingdom today (as well as South Africa) is the dominance of state churches and the cultural Christianity that arose out of western Christendom.

Nations that claim to be Christian lull their citizens into believing that they are Christians without personal regeneration and faith. Christendom creates the worst form of legalism since its "Christianity" is merely external. That external Christianity produces many blessings, but it is merely external, nonetheless. And we mustn't call something "Christian" that is merely conforming externally—that term must be reserved for those who are truly, internally regenerate. D. Martyn Lloyd-Jones emphasized the danger of this well:

> I would say that it is always wrong to talk about "Christianizing" anything. No such thing is possible, and I would describe that view as heretical. You are either a Christian, or you are not a Christian. It is only the Christian who can live the Christian life; it is only the Christian who can understand the Christian teaching. So whatever you may do to unregenerate individuals, and though you may change society's mode of living—and I am entirely in agreement with that—you must not use the term "Christianize." It is good to persuade people to live in a certain way, but you must not say they are living as Christians, because they cannot.[2]

As well-intentioned as we may be, and as many external goods come from it, we should not pretend as if unregenerate people are Christians.

It failed, because this is not what God has designed for human government in this present age. As we have seen, God instituted human government as a common grace institution to help to preserve peace and order in a sin-cursed world, not as an institution tasked with enforcing external conformity to all of God's moral law. That is the mission of the church through the Word by the power of the Spirit (more later).

---

[2] David Martyn Lloyd-Jones, *Romans: An Exposition of Chapter 13: Life in Two Kingdoms* (Carlisle, PA: Banner of Truth Trust, 2002), 143-44.

Furthermore, a fundamental reason Christendom has and always will fail is that human leaders are sinners—even Christian ones. C. S. Lewis pointed out the danger of theocracy as a form of government with sinful leaders:

> The loftier the pretensions of the power, the more meddlesome, inhuman and oppressive it will be. Theocracy is the worst of all possible governments. All political power is at best a necessary evil: but it is least evil when its sanctions are most modest and commonplace, when it claims no more than to be useful or convenient and sets itself strictly limited objectives. Anything transcendental or spiritual, or even anything very strongly ethical, in its pretensions is dangerous, and encourages it to meddle with our private lives.[3]

God has instituted human government for a very important purpose, and it is essential that we limit governmental authority to only that singular purpose.

Now let me be quick to answer some natural objections. I am *not* saying that Christians should stay out of the public sphere. We regenerate Christians ought to live out our biblical values in every sphere of life, promoting righteousness for the good of our fellow man. Like Israel in exile, we ought to "seek the welfare of the city where I

---

[3] C. S. Lewis, "Lilies That Fester," in *Essay Collection and Other Short Pieces* (New York: HarperCollins, 2000), 372.

have sent you into exile, and pray to the Lord on its behalf, for in its welfare you will find your welfare" (Jer 29:7). Nor am I saying that it doesn't matter how a Christian votes or what policies Christians support. Some politicians and policies are contrary to biblical teaching, and it would be a sin for Christians to support them.

A common objection is often something like, "Well, if you don't support Christian Nationalism, what kind of Nationalism do you want? Pagan Nationalism? Are you just going to be satisfied with drag queen story hours and increased oppression against Christians?" Of course not. We ought to grieve over "drag queen story hour," gay "marriage," and abortion, opposing them at every turn. We ought to call government to fulfill its God-appointed role of enforcing God's moral law to sustain civic order. We ought to live holy lives, demonstrate kindness toward all people, rear godly children, work hard, and apply what it means to be a Christian in whatever sphere God has called us.

But we do all of this as Christians in exile, expecting that "in the last days there will come times of difficulty.... Indeed, all who desire to live a godly life in Christ Jesus will be persecuted, while evil people and impostors will go on from bad to worse, deceiving and being deceived" (1 Tim 3:1, 12). We shouldn't desire persecution, but we should expect it, recognizing that actually a persecuted church is often a more pure church. "Cultural Christianity" is far less likely in a persecuted church.

The problem is that many Christians today are unwilling to be content with the tensions that God has ordained during this already/not yet period until Jesus comes again. We long for Christ's kingdom on earth, and that is a good longing. We ought to pursue the moral blessings of Christ's kingdom in our homes and in our churches. But God has not promised the blessings of Christ's kingdom for nations of unregenerate people. Those blessings will come when Jesus comes again and takes dominion over all, when every knee will bow to him—when every citizen of his earthly kingdom will also be a regenerate citizen of his heavenly kingdom.

Until Jesus comes again, we live in the tensions portrayed for us in the New Testament. Ultimately, we must recognize that the mandate given to us as churches is not to take dominion and establish Christendom; our mandate is to make disciples *from* every nation (Matt 28:19; cf. Rev 5:9), baptizing those who have been regenerated by the Spirit through the proclamation of the gospel, adding them to our number, and teaching them to observe everything Christ commanded.

CHRISTIAN RESPONSE TO HUMAN GOVERNMENT

So how ought we Christians live in light of the God-ordained institution of human government? The New Testament clearly defines our responsibilities.

First, as citizens of the common kingdom, we ought to submit to the human institutions that God has appointed. Remember, these human institutions are God's institutions. The common kingdom is God's kingdom. God established common institutions like family and government for the purpose of providentially ruling and sustaining humanity in a sin-cursed world. On that basis, we ought to submit to these common institutions that God has appointed. Paul says this succinctly:

> Let every person be subject to the governing authorities. For there is no authority except from God, and those that exist have been instituted by God. ² Therefore whoever resists the authorities resists what God has appointed, and those who resist will incur judgment. (Rom 13:1-2

Peter writes similarly in 1 Peter 2:13-17,

> Be subject for the Lord's sake to every human institution, whether it be to the emperor as supreme, ¹⁴ or to governors as sent by him to punish those who do evil and to praise those who do good. ¹⁵ For this is the will of God, that by doing good you should put to silence the ignorance of foolish people. ¹⁶ Live as people who are free, not using your freedom as a cover-up for evil, but living as servants of God. ¹⁷ Honor everyone. Love the brotherhood. Fear God. Honor the emperor.

As Jesus said in Matthew 22:21, "render to Caesar the things that are Caesar's." Notice what Peter says in 1 Peter 3:16—because we are citizens of the redemptive kingdom, we are free, but that doesn't mean we just throw off the governing authorities of the common kingdom that God has appointed, especially doing so to cover up evil in reality. We are to submit to and honor the governing authorities that God has instituted.

Now a couple important qualifications about this command. First, New Testament commands regarding human government were not given in a representative democratic republic. Christ, Paul, and Peter said these things in a Roman dictatorship. They did not say this in a situation where the governing officials were generally moral people, some of which even claimed to be Christian, like we have had historically in the United States. No, the emperor who Peter says to honor was very likely the infamous Nero. Various parts of Peter's letter indicate that the Christians to whom he was writing were already beginning to experience persecution from the government that would soon intensify.

The point is this: the command to submit to and honor governing authorities instituted by God is not dependent upon the moral goodness of the ruler but rather on the fact that God has instituted that ruler—as immoral and hostile to Christianity as he may be—for the purpose of sustaining order in the world. Peter says this in verse 14: God has appointed these governing authorities to punish evil and praise those who do good. When we submit to our governing authorities, we are submitting to God, and we are doing so for our own good.

However, there are limits to this submission. Jesus said, "render to Caesar the things that are Caesar's, and to God the things that are God's"—that's two kingdom theology in a nutshell. Often, these two commands do not conflict. But if they do, "we must obey God rather than men" (Acts 5:29). As we have already seen, this is where a healthy understanding of God's two kingdoms is helpful. We ought to recognize that the institutions God appointed for the common kingdom have been given specific jurisdictions, and that is where their authority ends. Paul says in Romans 13 that God gave human government the jurisdiction of punishing wrongdoing, especially violence, and that gives governments the authority to enact and enforce laws that prohibit violence against others. Paul also indicates in 1 Timothy 2:2 that governments ought to protect religious freedom, and both Peter and Paul indicate that governments should commend those who do good to others.

But government has not been given jurisdiction by God over education or health—that is the jurisdiction of the family. And the institution God appointed for the redemptive kingdom—the church—has been given specific jurisdictions. The church ought not meddle in matters under the jurisdiction of the family or government, but neither should the government meddle in matters under the jurisdiction of the church. Sometimes in discussions like this, this is called "sphere sovereignty."

So as Mark Snoeberger well articulated it:

> We must obey the government (1) unless the government explicitly tells us to disobey God, or (2) unless the government exceeds its jurisdiction so as to speak authoritatively into a sphere regulated by another, God-instituted authority.[4]

We also need to consider the fact that we do have a somewhat unique situation in a constitutional republic. We do not have a king. The president of the United States is not the equivalent to the emperor—the president has been elected by the people and has sworn to uphold the Constitution. In reality, the Constitution of the United States is the equivalent to the emperor in Peter's admonition.

So if the Constitution is our "emperor," what would it mean for us to honor the emperor? It would mean to uphold it. It's not perfect, but the emperor in Peter's day was not perfect either, to say the least. Our political situation is far better than what New Testament Christians had. We have the privilege of participation in our

---

[4] Mark Snoeberger, "How Can We Simultaneously 'Submit to Every Ordinance of Man' and 'Obey God Rather Than Men'?," *Detroit Baptist Theological Seminary* (blog), September 24, 2020, https://dbts.edu/2020/09/23/how-can-we-simultaneously-submit-to-every-ordinance-of-man-and-obey-god-rather-than-men/.

governmental system that New Testament Christians did not have. So in our situation, to honor the emperor means to vote, to be active in the political system, seeking to support candidates whose political policies will best accomplish what God has appointed as the purpose of government.

We can't just sit back and say, "We're citizens of another kingdom; so politics don't matter." No, *because* we are citizens of another kingdom, we *must* honor the emperor that our King appointed. So vote, stand for morality in our society, and be active in the political process for God's glory and, as Peter says in verse 17, for the honor of everyone and the love of the brotherhood.

Furthermore, Christians ought to be active in the sphere of government, seeking to encourage, and in some cases strongly advocate for, human governments to fulfill their God-ordained responsibilities under his sovereign rule. But when government exceeds its God-given role or advocates for activities that contradict God's moral law, Christians have a responsibility to speak up; and especially in a democratic republic, Christians ought to exercise their Constitutional rights to vote and advocate for leaders who will act properly in their role as servants of God.

Ultimately, however, we do not put our trust in princes, nor do we expect civil government to do what only the King of Kings will do when he comes again. As Sam Waldron helpfully argues,

Civil authority is not to be made the object of misdirected hope or consuming attention by the people of God. The mark of the perversion of the biblical perspective is the refocusing of hope on social change. This error pervades modern theologies of social change. The true hope of the people of God is the reestablishment of the theocratic kingdom. This, as the Scripture declares, will be the achievement not of civil reformation but of cataclysmic and supernatural divine intervention.[5]

Civil magistrates preserve peace and order in this present evil age, but true peace will come only when Jesus returns.

---

[5] Sam Waldron, *Political Revolution in the Reformed Tradition: A Historical and Biblical Critique* (Conway, AR: Free Grace Press, 2022), 113.

6

CULTURE MAKERS

A key implication of both the fact that God made man in his own image and that God blessed him is man's ability creatively organize God's creation into new creations. In the act of creating, we perhaps most perfectly image the Creator God. And at least one implication of God's blessing upon Adam of subduing the earth is to organize God's creation for the benefit of others. This act of taking what God has made and forming it into something else is what we call "culture." As Ken Myers has said, "Culture is what we make of creation."[1]

The importance for the issue at hand is to understand exactly what we are doing when people make culture, and especially how we as Christians ought to approach the matter of culture making in such a way that we are rightly reflecting our dual citizenship. In other words, the act of making culture is inherently good since it is part of God's image in us and his blessing upon us, but as citizens of the redemptive kingdom, we need to be sure that how we make culture reflects that ultimate citizenship.

---

[1] Ken Myers, *Mars Hill Audio Journal*, vol. 78, 2006.

INTERPRETING GOD'S NATURAL REVELATION

As we saw in chapter 3, God has revealed himself, both through what he has made—creation, and through what he has said—Scripture. But it is still up to human beings to *interpret* that revelation and then communicate it to others. We perceive God and his truth by means of both his natural revelation and his special revelation, but then we must properly interpret that revelation and arrive at the correction conclusions about God's reality.

Of course, depravity leads to the suppression of the truth. Man left to himself will wrongly interpret God's revelation, as we have already noted from Romans 1. This is the essence of the Fall—Satan took what God said and reinterpreted it to mean something contrary to what it really means. And ever since that time, sinful people have been misinterpreting the revelation of God, suppressing the truth by their unrighteousness. "Claiming to be wise, they became fools, and exchanged the glory of the immortal God for images resembling mortal man and birds and animals and creeping things" (Rom 1:22-23). They took what God made to be revelation of himself and creatively reshaped them into objects of worship to replace him.

This reveals the importance for Christians who make culture to be sure that what we make of what God made rightly reflects the God-intended meaning of his natural revelation. And the primary way we are able to do that is by interpreting God's natural revelation in light of his special revelation.

The critical point to recognize about culture making, then, is that all culture making is interpretation of God's natural revelation. An artist takes the stuff of God's creation—God's natural revelation—and creatively reorganizes it to emphasize a particular truth, shaping the listener or observer through that interpretation. Like a sermon is interpretation of God's Word, art is interpretation of God's world. Leland Ryken notes, "Art aims to convey not primarily the facts of life but the truth and meaning of those facts."[2] Art incarnates meaning in concrete form; it is the product of human creativity that expresses imaginative aspects of truth beyond mere fact.

LOOKING THROUGH

One of the last short stories C. S. Lewis wrote was called "Light." In the story a man named Robin, who was born blind, has recently had his sight restored through surgery. Robin finds himself quite disappointed with his restored sight, however, because he really wants to see that thing called "light" that he has heard so much about, and yet, while his wife and others insist that light is all around him, he can't *see* light. Weeks of being able to see but not being able to see light leads Robin to despair and

---

[2] Leland Ryken, *The Liberated Imagination: Thinking Christianly About the Arts* (Eugene, OR: Wipf & Stock, 2005), 26.

ultimately death. Of course, Robin's problem, and even the problem of his wife and others who could not manage to help him, was that light is not something we *see*; light is something *by which we see*.

Lewis's story is ultimately about the nature of human knowing, but it also illustrates well, I think, how we often approach the subject of beauty. In our post-Enlightenment era, beauty is something we look *at*; it is a subject we talk *about*; it is, perhaps, something we ought to learn to appreciate and enjoy.

However, as with light in Lewis's story, God's beauty is not merely something to think *about*, to look *at*, and to simply *recognize* or even *delight in*, but rather beauty is a significant way we come to know God and his world *through*. Or, to put it another way, beauty is not simply a category that stands alongside truth and goodness; rather, beauty is the means through which we come to really know what is true and good. This is so because beauty is not something we arbitrarily determine, beauty is inherently rooted in the nature and character of God, and he communicated beauty in what he made.

Belief in transcendent beauty is rooted in a conviction that God is the source, sustainer, and end of all things. The Bible clearly proclaims that God is self-existent and self-sustaining, and all things come from him (Rom 11:36). Everything that is true is so because God is Truth. Everything that is good is so because God is Good. And everything that is beautiful is so because God is

Beauty. There are no such things as brute facts apart from God; they are facts because God determined them to be so. There are no such things as moral standards that are merely conceived out of convention apart from God; actions are moral or immoral because God says they are. And in the same way, beauty is not in the eye of the beholder; something is beautiful when it reflects God who is beauty.

A Scripture passage that perhaps most clearly articulates this is Philippians 4:8:

> Finally, brethren, whatsoever things are true, whatsoever things are honest, whatsoever things are just, whatsoever things are pure, whatsoever things are lovely, whatsoever things are of good report; if there be any virtue, and if there be any praise, think on these things.

Here we find a list of absolute standards by which we must judge all things, including culture. The qualities listed as our standard could be grouped into three categories: truth, goodness, and beauty. Something is true when it corresponds to God's reality; something is good when it corresponds to God's morality; and something is beautiful when it is worthy of our delight as compared with God's beauty.

With this in mind, Christians as image-bearers of God must be committed to thinking God's thoughts after him, to behaving in certain ways that conform to God's moral will, and to loving those things that God calls lovely. Thoroughly Christian living is therefore concerned with orthodoxy—right belief, orthopraxy—right behavior, *and* orthopathy—right loves.

And yet the realm of orthopathy—right loving—is often missing from even the most robust Christian theology. We are all about rigorous doctrine, and we recognize our goal of cultivating thoroughly Christian values in every area of life, but do we recognize beauty as an essential means through which this will happen?

The primary, fundamental reason we ought to recognize the significance of beauty as a central means through which our loves are shaped and through which we really come to know God and his world is that the Bible itself is God's truth communicated in beautiful forms. God's Word is more than merely a collection of theological information. Instead, God's revelation of truth and goodness comes to us in various aesthetic forms such as narratives, poetry, and oratory that employ diverse aesthetic language.

These aesthetic forms are essential to the truth itself since God's inspired Word is exactly the best way that truth could be presented. Clyde S. Kilby observes, "The Bible comes to us in an artistic form which is often sublime, rather than as a document of practical, expository prose, strict in outline like a textbook." He asserts that these aesthetic forms are not merely decorative but part of the essential presentation of the Bible's truth: "We do not have truth and beauty, or truth decorated with beauty, or truth illustrated by the beautiful phrase, or truth in a 'beautiful setting.' Truth and beauty are in the Scriptures, as indeed they must always be, an inseparable unity."[3]

To put it another way—truth, goodness, and beauty, are three strands of a single cord that cannot be separated if we desire to truly know God and his world.

WHAT ACCORDS WITH SOUND DOCTRINE

This is why we must approach the matter of culture and the arts, which are part of God's common kingdom, from the perspective of those who are ultimately citizens of God's redemptive kingdom. Culture is not neutral; artistic expression is not neutral. As we have seen, culture is the product of human creativity such that we take what God has made, interpret that natural revelation, and then creatively communicate that interpretation by reorganizing what God is made into something new.

However, an artist's creative interpretation of God's natural revelation is subject to his humanity. As Ryken insists, "Since art not only presents experience but also interprets it—since it has ideational content and

---

[3] Clyde S. Kilby, *Christianity and Aesthetics* (Chicago: Inter-Varsity Press, 1961), 21.

embodies a world view or ethical outlook—it will always be open to classification as true or false."[4] Therefore, for Christians, making or evaluating culture must always be measured against God's special revelation.

A helpful text that helps articulate this idea is Titus 2:1: "But as for you, teach what accords with sound doctrine." What is Paul talking about here when he refers to "what accords with sound doctrine"? Is he talking about other intellectual truths that accord with doctrine. No, he tells us what kinds of things accord with sound doctrine in the following verses (vv 2-10). Some of what Paul lists there involve specific kinds of behavior, but most of what he lists as that which "accords with sound doctrine" or what "adorns the doctrine of God our Savior" (v 10) involve inward qualities like sobriety, dignity, reverence, self-control, integrity, steadfastness, and purity.

But here's the thing: these are inward qualities that in many ways are difficult to precisely define or articulate. Take reverence, for example. What is it? Clearly there must be an objective reality called "reverence," but how would you define it? It's difficult, right?

Yet the difficulty in describing a character quality does not render it subjective. God commands us to be characterized by reverence, dignity, and self-control— these are what "accord with sound doctrine." So we have a responsibility to discern what these qualities are like and cultivate them in our lives. These are applications of

---

[4] Ryken, *The Liberated Imagination*, 196.

sound doctrine (words) in life behavior (works).

So how do we both communicate and cultivate these kinds of non-verbal qualities to others? This is the power of art. Scripture itself embodies and communicates these kinds of qualities like reverence and dignity through the artistic imagery it employs in the communication of God's truth—Scripture itself artistically embodies sound doctrine. It is filled with imagery, poetry, narrative, and other artistic devices that do communicate truth through propositions, but Scripture also communicates embodied qualities that accord with sound doctrine through artistic imagery. As Ryken observes, "Everything that is communicated in a piece of writing is communicated through the forms in which it is embodied."[5]

So Scripture commands us to be reverent, and then various artistic elements in Scripture *show* us what reverence is like. Scripture tells us to love God, and then its artistic expressions *embody* appropriate love. Scripture admonishes us to be godly, and its artistic expressions *form our conception* of what godliness should be like.

EMBODYING GOD'S TRUTH, GOODNESS, AND BEAUTY

This is the importance of culture making for Christians. Through creating art, Christians are able to communicate

---

[5] Leland Ryken, *Words of Delight: A Literary Introduction to the Bible*, 2nd ed. (Grand Rapids: Baker Academic, 1993), 20.

and cultivate interpretations of God's world that accord with sound doctrine through beauty.

Art embodies qualities in the way we have been discussing because as we have seen, art presents an interpretation of the ideas it carries. As Ryken notes,

> Artists do more than present human experience; they also interpret it from a specific perspective. *Works of art make implied assertions about reality.*[6]

How so? In exactly the same way that reverence, dignity, and self-control *accord with* sound doctrine. Reverence is not just another way of articulating sound doctrine—reverence *embodies* sound doctrine; it applies sound doctrine in real life.

In the same way, art can embody ideas. Ryken explains:

> The method of art is to incarnate meaning in concrete form. *The artist shows*, and is never content to only tell in the form of propositions. The strategy of art is to enact rather than summarize.[7]

This makes sense when we remember that art—whether we're talking about poetry, literature, drama, or music—is itself human behavior; art is human expression. What

---

[6] Ryken, *The Liberated Imagination*, 26.
[7] Ryken, *The Liberated Imagination*, 28.

we express through an artistic medium is not just ideas abstractly stated; rather, an artistic expression *is a person's interpretation of ideas in concrete forms.*

Therefore, we must recognize that all cultural expression, whether produced by citizens of God's common kingdom or citizens of God's redemptive kingdom, embodies implied interpretations of God's revelation. And so, we Christians must always ask about any work of culture:

> Does the interpretation of reality in this work conform or fail to conform to Christian doctrine?[8]

In other words, do the qualities embodied in this work of art accord with sound doctrine?

I am afraid that most Christians do not recognize this, and this is evidenced at very least by the fact that many Christians are afraid to affirm and defend absolute beauty in the same way we do absolute truth and morality. We have bought into the modernist idea that beauty is in the eye of the beholder, and the postmodern multicultural agenda that argues art is merely neutral contextualization of a given civilization. We still view beauty and the arts as means to the end of making truth interesting instead of as ends in themselves. We view beauty as something to *see* rather than something *by which we see.*

I phrase it that way specifically because again, often

---

[8] Ryken, *The Liberated Imagination*, 179.

when we consider aesthetics, it becomes something we talk *about* and think *about*. Talking about, thinking about, and looking at beauty are all good as far as they go, but works of beauty—that which shapes our loves and cultivates virtue in us—is not something to look *at* but rather what we see *through*.

By aesthetics, I am referring to the very broad idea that finds its roots in the Greek word *aisthanomai*, which means, "I perceive, feel, sense." Aesthetics involves all that affects perception. It involves the *how* ideas are expressed and communicated. It certainly includes a consideration of beauty and art, but it is far more than that. Every way in which we learn, every way in which we encounter truth aesthetically shapes the way we perceive the truth. Aesthetic form is the container in which we perceive truth, and the truth takes the shape of the container such that perception of the truth is affected by the container.

So the power of aesthetics is that everything about the forms through which we perceive truth forms us to know and love God and his world through renewed eyes.

The apostle Paul prays for this very kind of renewal in Philippians 1:9-11, when he says,

> And it is my prayer that your love may abound more and more, with knowledge and all discernment, so that you may approve what is excellent, and so be pure and blameless for the day of Christ, filled with

the fruit of righteousness that comes through Jesus Christ, to the glory and praise of God.

Paul knows that what truly characterizes a Christian is love, what he describes in the previous verse as "the affection of Christ Jesus." Jesus himself taught that the greatest commandment is to love the Lord your God with all your heart and with all your soul and with all your mind and with all your strength.

But this love is not the romanticized sentimentalism so characteristic of our day. Notice in particular how Paul characterizes this love—"love with knowledge and discernment." Here, perhaps, is an apt description of the goal of Christian sanctification—that your love may abound more and more, with knowledge and discernment so that you may approve what is excellent, and so be pure and blameless for the day of Christ, filled with the fruit of righteousness that comes through Jesus Christ, to the glory and praise of God.

What Paul prays for here is a love characterized by "full knowledge," knowledge of God and his world, knowledge of his works through history, knowledge of his Word. But Christian love is not characterized by knowledge alone, and likewise the goal of Christian sanctification is not simply knowledge. What does Paul say: "And it is my prayer that your love may abound more and more, with knowledge, *and all discernment.*" There's the other half of Christian love; there's the other half of the goal of your sanctification, and indeed what you must pursue in the entirety of your life, including the common grace aspects of culture and the arts. This is the biblical virtue of wisdom, the ability to take all of the knowledge we have gleaned about God and his world and then discern how other elements *fit* into the larger whole, whether they be ways of life, personal experiences, events happening around us—wisdom is the ability to discern what *fits* in God's design for the world and what does not fit.

The cultivation of knowledge *and* discernment is the aim of Christian sanctification because it prepares us for a life of properly fitting together all of the particular information we will encounter around us into the larger whole as God intends. There are many people who have accumulated a lot of knowledge, but relatively few who truly know what to do with that knowledge, who have the ability to perceive how that knowledge fits together properly. As Paul continues to say in Philippians 1, "so that you may approve what is excellent." That's wisdom. That's discernment.

Now here's the fascinating thing about this little word "discernment" in Philippians 1:9. "Discernment" is a translation of the Greek word *aisthanomai*—from which we get the English word "aesthetics."

This reveals the important, fundamental purpose behind beauty in Christian sanctification and why, therefore, culture is not neutral. The aesthetic elements of the common kingdom are not merely value-added; they are not included merely to make the acquisition of knowledge more engaging or interesting. The aesthetic elements of our sanctification are fundamentally *moral* because they help *form* discernment within us—they help form *wisdom*. This is the formative power of beauty.

THE EYES OF YOUR HEART

Now how, exactly, does beauty form wisdom? I'd like to highlight two ways that beautiful cultural expressions can and should form within us a capacity to see God's order and beauty in his world.

First, beautiful works of the imagination form our capacity to properly perceive fittingness in God's world. Beauty *is* fittingness, and so when we immerse ourselves in beauty—in works of art and means of communication that manifest a profound fittingness in God's world as he has intended, our moral imaginations are shaped as to what is fitting in the created order.

One of my favorite paintings on display at the national gallery in Washington D.C. is a work called "Fanny/Fingerpainting" by Chuck Close. If you turned the corner in the gallery and encountered the painting up close, all you would see would be a mess of fingerprints. Apparent randomness and disorder. But as you back away from the painting, you would behold a stunningly detailed portrait of an old woman that looks photo realistic. What appeared up close to be random disorder actually fits in much larger beautiful whole.

This kind of phenomenon characterizes all beautiful art to one degree or another in an almost endless variety of ways. A moment of musical dissonance frozen in time seems harsh and purposeless, but conceived as but a moment in a larger musical composition, we begin to understand how the parts fit into a beautiful whole. One gesture of the body alone may seem awkward, but together with other complementary gestures, it creates a beautifully graceful dance.

By studying and immersing ourselves in, and especially performing, truly beautiful works of art like these, we are developing wisdom, the ability to perceive a part—a moment frozen in time—and discern how that part fits in the whole of God's all-wise and beautiful plan for his world.

And likewise, second, beauty in worship orients us to what is fitting in our relationship to God and his world. As Vanhoozer observes,

> Both great art and worship awaken our senses and imaginations to the contours of the created order. Yet, unlike art, worship engrafts us into the drama of redemption, into that Trinitarian design for life in which beauty is a loving consent toward another.[9]

---

[9] Kevin J. Vanhoozer, *Pictures at a Theological Exhibition: Scenes of*

The beauty of gospel-shaped, covenant-renewal worship[10] regularly orients us to the drama of redemption, enabling us with enlightened eyes to perceive God's work in the world for his glory and the glory of his people. Beautiful liturgy and music orders our affections into what Lewis called "stable sentiments."[11] Worship that liturgically participates in the real worship of heaven realigns us with that true reality.

Citizens of God's redemptive kingdom cannot approach culture and the arts within God's common kingdom as if those things are neutral. Beauty is not optional, incidental, or simply for valueless entertainment. Beauty is what forms within us true love with knowledge and all discernment. True beauty equips us to navigate the complexities of life in God's world; beauty makes us wise.

Our world is filled with ugliness, disorder, chaos, and pain. Considered as frozen moments in time, such realities might cause us to despair if we cannot perceive how these moments of ugliness fit into an ordered plan of a sovereign God. But having the eyes of our hearts enlightened, having gained through beautiful art "the ability to grasp meaningful patterns or conceive unified wholes out of apparently unrelated elements," we are better able

---

the Church's Worship, Witness and Wisdom (Downers Grove: IVP Academic, 2016), 139.

[10] For more on this, see my book, Biblical Foundations of Corporate Worship (Conway, AR: Free Grace Press, 2022).

[11] C. S Lewis, The Abolition of Man (New York: HarperOne, 2001), 24–25.

to "'see' God and the kingdom of God at work in the world."[12]

---

[12] Vanhoozer, *Pictures at a Theological Exhibition*, 27.

7

THE CHURCH'S MISSION

We have been considering God's plan to govern all things in this present age through two kingdoms—he instituted common human institutions like family and government for all humankind to maintain order and peace in a sinful world, and he instituted his redeemed people who are ruled by Christ, strive to live holy lives, and seek to gather more redeemed people through the proclamation of the gospel. During this age, we Christians are dual citizens—we are still part of the common kingdom as human beings, but we are also citizens of the redemptive kingdom because of our relationship to Christ. One day, these two kingdoms will be united into one eternal kingdom after Jesus comes again.

One significant implication of a biblical understanding of God's two kingdoms is that when we think about our responsibility toward the culture around us, we need to distinguish between our responsibilities as individual Christians who are part of God's universal common kingdom on the one hand, and the responsibilities of churches as a called out community of God's redemptive kingdom on the other. We must recognize, for instances, that not everything Scripture commands of Christians as individuals applies in the same way to local churches as institutions. To cite an obvious example that Kevin DeYoung and Greg Gilbert use in their very helpful book on the subject, *What is the Mission of the Church?*, Christ's command for a Christian husband to love his wife as his own body does not extend to a church as a whole. DeYoung and Gilbert rightly point out that there is a difference between "the church organic," that is, Christians living life together within the community, and "the church institutional," the local gathering of believers who covenant together to fulfill very specific responsibilities given by Christ to local churches.[1] These responsibilities have been given to churches "when you come together" (1 Cor 11); they are responsibilities not given to individual Christians when they are alone or even to groups of Christians who are not gathered together formally as a local church.

We have already given focused attention to how we as Christians ought to live as citizens of the earthly common kingdom in our roles within families and societies. As we have seen, God instituted these spheres for *all people* (not just redeemed people) for the good order of human life.

However, though as Christians we are citizens of an earthly kingdom, that is not our ultimate citizenship. As

---

[1] Kevin DeYoung and Greg Gilbert, *What Is the Mission of the Church? Making Sense of Social Justice, Shalom, and the Great Commission* (Wheaton: Crossway, 2011), 232.

Christians, and particularly as *churches*, our primary identity and mission is redemptive. Therefore, in this chapter I would like to focus our attention on the responsibilities of gathered churches.

CHRIST'S AUTHORITY

Christ promised in his prayer to the Father in John 17 that he would give his disciples—and, by extension, the church they would establish—a mission; he prayed, "As you sent me into the world, so I have sent them into the world" (Jn 17:18). After his resurrection, he said something similar to his disciples in John 21:21: "As the Father has sent me, even so I am sending you. Sending implies authority. The Father sent the Son into the world, and so Jesus's mission was to obey what his Father had commanded him to do. In John 4:34, Jesus said, "My food is to do the will of him who sent me and to accomplish his work." In John 5:30 he said, "I can do nothing on my own. As I hear, I judge, and my judgment is just, because I seek not my own will but the will of him who sent me." In John 6:38 he said, "For I have come down from heaven, not to do my own will but the will of him who sent me." Jesus was on earth to do what the Father commanded him. And remember, in some way that I don't pretend to understand, Jesus did not *want* to go to the cross; he asked the Father to take that cup away from him. But at the end of the day he said, "Not my will, but yours be done."

And in a parallel way, Jesus sent his disciples, and sending implies authority. The fact that he sent them means they must obey what he commands them to do.

This is why Jesus begins his final address to his disciples in Matthew 28:18 this way:

> And Jesus came and said to them, "All authority in heaven and on earth has been given to me."

He is about to give them their commission, and he does so on the basis of his authority over them. This authority is rooted in his divinity to be sure, but it is actually even more than that. Remember what Jesus's life, death, and resurrection accomplished: Jesus the Son of Man, the Second Adam, succeeded in being the perfect king/priest where Adam had failed. This earned him the right to rule, not just the right to rule as God over his universal kingdom—the Son of God always had that right; Jesus's obedience to his Father earned him the right to rule as the Son of Man over the redemptive kingdom. The term in Matthew 28:18 translated "authority" means "the right to rule." Because Jesus "humbled himself by becoming obedient to the point of death, even death on a cross, ... God has highly exalted him and bestowed on him the name that is above every name, so that at the name of Jesus every knee should bow, in heaven and on earth and under the earth, and every tongue confess that Jesus Christ is Lord, to the glory of God the Father" (Phil 2:8-11).

This is what David prophesied in Psalm 110 when he said, "The Lord says to my Lord, Sit at my right hand, until I make your enemies your footstool." Right after Matthew 28:20, Jesus ascended into heaven, where he is now seated at the right hand of the Father, having earned the right to rule over all. That right to rule over all things will not be fully realized until after all things are put in subjection under his feet. Hebrews 2:8–9 states,

> At present, we do not yet see everything in subjection to him. [9] But we see him who for a little while was made lower than the angels, namely Jesus, crowned with glory and honor because of the suffering of death, so that by the grace of God he might taste death for everyone.

But the fact that Christ *has* earned the right to rule through his death and resurrection means that he *does* have special authority *particularly* over citizens of the redemptive kingdom. Christ rules the church. Ephesians 2:20 says that Christ is the church's cornerstone. Christ sent his disciples with a commission because he has authority over his redeemed people, the church.

It is important to recognize at this point that Jesus's authority as the Redeemer King over his church is different than his authority as Sovereign King over all things. The triune God has always and will always have authority as Sovereign over all things. Jesus Christ's unique rule as

Redeemer King is at present only true for people he has redeemed. But that is a critical point to remember: we who are redeemed—Christ's church—must obey what he has commanded us to do as his church. To do less than what he has commanded, *or to do more than what he has commanded*, is a failure to submit to his redemptive authority over us.

APOSTOLIC AUTHORITY

So as Christ's church, how do we know what he wants us to do? Well, this is why we must notice to whom Jesus is giving this commission—he is commissioning his eleven disciples (and later the twelfth—Paul), giving them derivative authority over the church. Jesus Christ is the cornerstone of the church, Paul says in Ephesians 2, but the apostles and prophets are the foundation (v. 20). The apostles to which Paul refers are these eleven plus Paul, who were called by Christ himself, taught by Christ himself, personally witnessed Christ risen from the dead, were given direct revelation from God, and were affirmed by God through signs and wonders. These twelve, a few of which penned the New Testament epistles, were the foundation of the church; in other words, Christ rules his church *through* his apostles. To obey the apostles is to obey Christ, and to ignore them is to ignore their Master.

The apostles have authority over the church, not because they were particularly special or wise, but rather because Christ spoke through them. Christ had promised them that he would bring his words to their remembrance (Jn 14:26) through the Spirit's ministry, who would guide them into truth (Jn 16:13). Paul said in Galatians 1:11, "For I would have you know, brothers, that the gospel that was preached by me is not man's gospel"—it is Christ's gospel. In 1 Corinthians 11, when giving the church instructions about how to observe the Lord's Supper, Paul says, "For I received from the Lord what I also delivered to you."

NEW TESTAMENT AUTHORITY

Those apostles received teaching from Christ himself, and then they wrote down their authoritative teaching "as they were carried along by the Holy Spirit" (2 Pet 1:21), which became the New Testament Scriptures that Paul would describe as literally "breathed out by God" (2 Tim 3:16). This is why Paul could say in 1 Thessalonians 2:13 that what he wrote to the churches is the Word of God. In 1 Corinthians 14:37–38, Paul states, "If anyone thinks that he is a prophet, or spiritual, he should acknowledge that the things I am writing to you are a command of the Lord. If anyone does not recognize this, he is not recognized." Since the apostles are representatives of Christ himself, their inspired writings carry his authority.

So why is this important when thinking about our responsibilities as Christ's church? When Jesus says, "All authority has been given to me," that authority is exercised through his apostles, and specifically through what they wrote in the pages of the New Testament. Furthermore, since Jesus affirmed his authority as the basis for the commission he was about to give his apostles as the foundation of the church, what those apostles wrote is the only authoritative instruction concerning how the gathered church is supposed to operate. As part of Christ's redemptive kingdom, gathered churches *must* do what Christ commands us to do, and we must not add anything to what Christ commanded us to do.

As we saw previously, God has revealed himself generally to all people through what he has made: "The heavens declare the glory of God, and the sky above proclaims his handiwork" (Ps 19:1). This is God's natural revelation given to all people:

> For his invisible attributes, namely, his eternal power and divine nature, have been clearly perceived, ever since the creation of the world, in the things that have been made. So they are without excuse. (Rom 1:20)

This general revelation of God is the basis for all aspects of God's common kingdom. But when it comes to God's redemptive kingdom—when it comes to a saving knowledge of Christ and how we should operate when we gather together as Christ's church, God's general revelation is insufficient. Rather, it is God's special revelation—

his inspired Word—that governs what we do specifically as the redeemed people of God.

And even more specifically, though it is true that the Old Testament is absolutely inspired, authoritative, and profitable for us, the New Testament, especially the epistles, are the specific apostolic instruction that Christ has given to us as the most focused authority for what we do as churches. This is the nature of God's progressive revelation. Hebrews 1:1-2 succinctly summarize this important doctrine:

> Long ago, at many times and in many ways, God spoke to our fathers by the prophets, [2] but in these last days he has spoken to us by his Son, whom he appointed the heir of all things, through whom also he created the world.

All Scripture is inspired, authoritative, profitable, and sufficient, but not all in the same way. For example, are the Mosaic dietary restrictions profitable? Sure, but not in the same way as Paul's discussion of dietary restrictions in Colossians 2. This is because God is progressively accomplishing his plan to establish his kingdom on earth, and thus the revelation he gave us in each successive administration of his plan is also progressive.

The supreme authority for what the New Testament church is and how we are supposed to conduct ourselves in this stage in the outworking of God's plan must come from the New Testament, particularly the epistles. Edward Hiscox says it this way:

> The New Testament is the constitution of Christianity, the charter of the Christian Church, the only authoritative code of ecclesiastical law, and the warrant and justification of all Christian institutions.[2]

Furthermore, we must also remember that not all of the commands given even in the New Testament are for gathered churches; as I've already mentioned, some commands are given to churches "when you come together," and other commands are given to individuals, such as "husbands, love your wives." Thus, it is very important that we carefully consider the central mission that Christ has given through his apostles for gathered New Testament churches.

THE CHURCH'S COMMISSION

On that important basis, then, what is the mission Christ has given to his redeemed people gathered into local churches?

> Go therefore and make disciples of all nations, baptizing them in the name of the Father and of the Son

---

[2] Edward T. Hiscox, *The New Directory for Baptist Churches* (Valley Forge, PA: Judson, 1894), 11.

and of the Holy Spirit, [20] teaching them to observe all that I have commanded you. And behold, I am with you always, to the end of the age. (Matt 28:19-20)

Churches as formal, local institutions have been given a very specific, singular mission in this age, best articulated in the Great Commission of Matthew 28. You'll notice that there are several phrases in this text that sound like commands, but grammatically there is actually only one command: "Make disciples" is the mandate Christ gave to his church—nothing more and nothing less. All of the rest of the phrases in this passage that sound in English like commands, which we'll consider in a moment, actually further explain the central command. In fact, we could even say that all of the commands and discussion throughout the rest of the New Testament that directly relate to the church are simply giving further explanation or correcting errors related to the central command of making disciples. All of that explanation and correction still carries with it the force of a command, but it all comes back to this central command: make disciples.

So what is a disciple? Well, a disciple of Christ is simply a follower of Christ. He is one who obeys Christ's commands, not simply out of duty, but because he knows, if you love Christ, you will do what he commands (Jn 14:15). And the Great Commission bears this out in verse 20 where it says that part of what it means to make disciples is "teaching them to observe all that I have commanded you." A disciple is someone who observes Christ's commands, who submits to his rule. To put it another way, a disciple is a citizen of the redemptive kingdom.

Now we might say, "Isn't worship our first priority? Why isn't our primary mission as churches to worship?" Well keep in mind, to be a disciple *is* to worship God. Submission to the rule of Christ and obedience to his commands *is* worship. Don't think of obedience to Christ as distinct from loving Christ. I alluded to John 14:15 earlier; Jesus said, "If you love me"—if you worship me—"you will keep my commandments." To be a disciple of Christ is to worship Christ. So we could think of it this way: our mission is to make disciple-worshipers. The ultimate aim of all things is the worship and glory of God, but our specific mission as churches is to disciple worshipers for God's glory.

But sinners can't worship God—sinners cannot submit to Christ's rule; so in order to make disciples who observe Christ's commands, there are a couple more preliminary steps. First, in the parallel passage in Mark, Christ presents the first step toward making disciples: "Go into all the world and proclaim the gospel to the whole creation" (Mark 16:15). Citizenship in the redemptive kingdom—being a disciple of Jesus Christ—requires first that someone hear the good news, repent of their sins, and trust in Christ for salvation. So, the first necessary step in making disciples is proclamation of the gospel.

Second, Christ commands that new believers must be baptized. Physical water baptism is an outward visible sign of inward Spirit baptism. Spirit baptism happens at the moment of conversion and unites us to Christ (1 Cor 12:13)—it makes us citizens of the redemptive kingdom. Water baptism is a public profession of faith and unites us to a visible church—the visible representation of the redemptive kingdom.

And the third necessary component of making disciples is teaching them to observe all that Christ commanded. This is the clear teaching and preaching of Scripture, again all of Scripture, but especially the apostolic teaching recorded in the New Testament.

SPIRITUAL MISSION

Now we could go into further detail on each of these components of making disciples, and that certainly would have great profit. But for our purposes here, I want to note a couple important points about this commission as it relates to our responsibility as churches in the world.

First, notice that with regard to churches, that is, to gatherings of citizens of the redemptive kingdom, our mission is exclusively redemptive in nature: make disciples. Our mission involves gathering more citizens of the redemptive kingdom through evangelism, baptism, and teaching. The church's mission is entirely spiritual in nature—it does not involve temporal earthly matters that belong to the common kingdom. As Michael Vlach helpfully observes, "The church's primary responsibility in this age is gospel proclamation and making disciples. . . . The church's mission is not cultural or societal transformation."[3] The only mandate given to churches that involves physical matters is "contributing to the needs of the saints" (Rom 12:13), but even then, only when the common institution of the family breaks down (1 Tim 5:3-8). Never is the church given the responsibility of meeting the physical needs of society at large. That is the responsibility of institutions in the common kingdom.

Neither is the church given any commands regarding political involvement. We are to pray "for kings and all who are in high positions," but churches should not in any official capacity hold political rallies, endorse candidates, or advocate for specific policy positions. Note that even in a very oppressive governmental situation, the New Testament never advocates for churches attempting to overthrow tyrannical governments and establish more righteous governments. That is not the mission of the church. The church's mission is purely spiritual.

This is important exactly because of the issue of authority that we discussed earlier. When the church is operating as a church, it must do what its authority commanded it to do, no more and no less. If our authority as churches is what Christ commanded through his

---

[3] Michael J. Vlach, *He Will Reign Forever: A Biblical Theology of the Kingdom of God* (Silverton, OR: Lampion Press, 2017), 541.

apostles, then we may only do what can follow "Thus says the Lord."

Now notice that I have been very careful to say "churches" here. I am not saying that individual Christians may not be involved in politics or meet physical needs in society or other cultural matters. Again, this is why we must carefully distinguish between individual Christians in the common kingdom and gathered churches as part of the redemptive kingdom. These are two distinct kingdoms of God with different citizenships, different responsibilities, and different forms of God's revelation as their authority. As we have already seen, the New Testament does give very clear direction for how individual Christians are to behave as members of society, but gathered *churches* have a distinctly spiritual mission of making disciples.

DISCIPLING COMMON KINGDOM CITIZENS

Nevertheless, because members of churches may certainly be involved in various cultural endeavors as citizens of the common kingdom, the church does have a secondary role in cultural engagement: churches should instruct believers in what it means to live Christianly in society. Part of what it means to fulfill the Great Commission is to teach Christians how to live out the implications of their relationship with God and how to obey the Great

Commandments through being holy, active citizens in society for the good of their fellow man. Churches should speak to relevant moral issues under attack in society as part of discipling Christians to know how they should live in that society. However, churches must not speak beyond Scripture, may not require of their people what Scripture does not require, and should not in any official capacity meddle in civil affairs.

You might say, "But if these political or social issues are important, then why shouldn't we as a church make them a primary emphasis?" This is a good question, because we don't want to fall into the other ditch of saying that none of these issues in culture matter, and we should just stay silent. They do matter. But if we as gathered churches make them our primary emphasis, inevitably the mission that Christ has given us gets sidelined. You begin to hear things like, "Preach the gospel; use words if necessary." The implication is that we preach the gospel *through* doing good in society, not through clear, bold proclamation. This is the social gospel, and when you buy into the social gospel, you lose the true gospel.

Churches should certainly stand up for truth and condemn antibiblical ideologies or immorality within the broader society, but there is even a danger here. We must always remember that the primary way churches fight against antibiblical aspects of the society is by making disciples. If we think that the primary way to battle unbiblical conduct is through political schemes, or if fighting against immorality itself becomes our mission, then we lose the gospel, and we actually lose the mission Christ has given us.

This runs contrary to how many evangelicals think. Very prominent leaders within evangelicalism teach that churches should be actively engaged in social, cultural, and political affairs, seeking to do "kingdom work" through "cultural transformation." Hopefully you recognize the problems with this. This thinking blurs the distinction between the common kingdom and the redemptive kingdom, and it goes beyond what the New Testament clearly commands as the church's mission. Nowhere does the New Testament command churches to transform or "redeem" culture, engage in political activism, or solve physical problems. The church's responsibility is to make disciples.

And the reverse is true as well: institutions of the common kingdom ought not meddle in the affairs of the church. Governments, for example, have been instituted by God specifically for the purpose of protecting innocent life, but governments have no authority over churches. Evangelicals who blur the distinction tend to err in this point too, allowing the government to dictate what their churches can and cannot do. "Render to Caesar the things that are Caesar's," Christ said, "and to God the things that are God's." The church's authority is Christ alone, explained through apostolic teaching recorded in God's special revelation.

RESTRAINT

Third, churches may indeed have an influence upon culture due to the fact that the Holy Spirit of God is active in the world through the church in a manner unique to this present age. Paul teaches in 2 Thessalonians 2:6-7 that the Holy Spirit is currently restraining "the lawless one" through his indwelling ministry in the church. This also relates to Christ's description of his followers as "the salt of the earth," those who, through living in "peace with one another" can serve to preserve righteousness in the world (Matt 5:13; Mark 9:50).

With this perspective, the church may have a restraining or preserving influence on broader culture to one degree or another, but this is through what James Davison Hunter calls "faithful presence" within the world.[4] Rather than this being a particular political strategy or set of cultural programs, this kind of restraint or preservation is accomplished by churches discipling believers to live Spirit-controlled lives, and through Christians submitting to the sanctifying work of the Spirit in every aspect of life, simply living in unity together as separated Christians in society. In this way, Christians are salt and light, helping through example and act to restrain human depravity in the surrounding culture. We are

---

[4] James Davison Hunter, *To Change the World: The Irony, Tragedy, and Possibility of Christianity in the Late Modern World* (Oxford: Oxford University Press, 2010).

participating as citizens in the human institutions created by God for the purpose of ordering the natural world and providing restraints upon human sinfulness, not accomplishing "redemptive kingdom work."

The fact of the matter is that Scripture never promises societal transformation in this age. Things might get better for a time, but usually because more people have come to faith in Christ, not because of some sort of social or political program. And things will get worse; as Paul predicts in 2 Timothy 3:12-13, "Indeed, all who desire to live a godly life in Christ Jesus will be persecuted, while evil people and impostors will go on from bad to worse, deceiving and being deceived." When things get bad, it should sadden us, but it should not surprise us.

But neither should we get discouraged. Remember, it is not our responsibility to succeed where Adam failed; Christ has already done that, and his perfect rule will come to pass only when he comes again. In the meantime, we seek to make disciples and live holy lives.

TO THE END OF THE AGE

Finally, notice how Christ ends the commission: "And behold, I am with you always, to the end of the age" (Matt 28:20). Christ is the church's authority—it is *his* church, but that also means he won't leave us. It's his mission, and so he will see that it comes to pass. We are responsible to make disciples, but Christ will build his church.

And he will do so until the end of the age, when he comes again in glory to unite the two kingdoms into one perfect eternal kingdom. Then there will be no distinction: the common and redemptive will be united in subjection under the perfect king. And we will live in obedience to him and worship him perfectly for all eternity.

8

WORSHIP IS WARFARE

The Bible uses several different metaphors to describe our lives as Christians in this present age. It describes us as pilgrims and exiles, as a priesthood, as a holy nation, and as a building. It describes us like farmers and ambassadors and athletes. One of the most prevalent images of the Christian life is one of warfare.

> Put on the whole armor of God, that you may be able to stand against the schemes of the devil. (Eph 6:11)

> Beloved, I urge you as sojourners and exiles to abstain from the passions of the flesh, which wage war against your soul. (1 Pet 2:11)

> Share in suffering as a good soldier of Christ Jesus. (2 Tim 2:3)

> This charge I entrust to you, Timothy, my child, in accordance with the prophecies previously made about you, that by them you may wage the good warfare. (1 Tim 1:18)

Fight the good fight of the faith. (1 Tim 6:12)

In 2 Corinthians 10, Paul uses this image of warfare as well, but he contrasts the spiritual warfare of Christians with the physical warfare of common kingdoms:

> I, Paul, myself entreat you, by the meekness and gentleness of Christ—I who am humble when face to face with you, but bold toward you when I am away!—² I beg of you that when I am present I may not have to show boldness with such confidence as I count on showing against some who suspect us of walking according to the flesh. ³ For though we walk in the flesh, we are not waging war according to the flesh. ⁴ For the weapons of our warfare are not of the flesh but have divine power to destroy strongholds. ⁵ We destroy arguments and every lofty opinion raised against the knowledge of God, and take every thought captive to obey Christ, ⁶ being ready to punish every disobedience, when your obedience is complete. (2 Cor 10:1-6)

Paul is writing here about the necessity to battle against false teachers within the church. He is describing a battle strategy for Christian warfare. And in describing his war strategy, Paul gives us today an important battle plan for how citizens of the redemptive kingdom ought to engage in the war as well.

THE AUTHORITY OF OUR WARFARE

Paul begins with a phrase that we may be just tempted to skip over, but the emphasis with which he phrases his opening is notable: "I, Paul, myself entreat you." Paul has defended his ministry in the previous nine chapters, and he is about to engage in some very direct rebuke to the remaining minority in the Corinthian church who are still sowing discord. And so he begins by establishing his authority: I, Paul, myself.

Paul is an apostle of Jesus Christ, and as an apostle, Paul had the delegated authority of Christ. Paul is asserting his authority as an apostle. This is particularly important for Paul here, because the very people he is about to confront in the Corinthian church claimed to be apostles—super-apostles in fact (11:5), but they were false apostles (11:13). And they were challenging Paul's authority as an apostle.

There are no apostles today, but this opening does provide an important foundation for all ministry warfare in the present age, because as we discussed in the last chapter, we do have apostolic authority in our day inscripturated in the pages of the New Testament. Acts 2:42 tells us that the early Christians devoted themselves to the apostles' doctrine. They recognized the authority of the apostles' teaching.

In other words, Paul begins his discussion of Christian warfare by asserting his authority as an apostle of Jesus Christ, and we have that same foundation for our warfare, not in ourselves, but in the authoritative, sufficient Word of God. And this is important, because as we discuss our warfare, it is critically important that the *authority* for our warfare be in the right place. The authority for our warfare is not in any man or any movement, our authority is in the inspired Word of God alone.

THE CHARACTER OF OUR WARFARE

After establishing the authority for his warfare, Paul next describes the character of warfare he is engaging. Notice that he begins by saying, "I entreat you." I *beg* you (v2). Paul is about to use some very direct language and describe the Christian life as one of warfare, but he doesn't start there. He entreats his readers, "by the meekness and gentleness of Christ." Paul knew he had to battle against these enemies of Christ stirring up trouble in the church, but he did not want to.

Paul is determined to confront these false apostles directly in these last three chapters of this letter, but he begins gently. He doesn't want to have another confrontational visit. He says in verse 2, "I beg of you that when I am present I may not have to show boldness with such confidence as I count on showing against some who suspect us of walking according to the flesh." Paul doesn't want to have to boldly confront them, but clearly he is willing to do so if they don't heed his warnings. He is saying in effect, "Don't mistake my compassion for weakness; I will come with a rod if I have to," just like he had said previously in 1 Corinthians. And how he's having to say the same thing again to this remaining minority of false teachers in the church. But he would rather they listen to his words here in the last three chapters and repent than for him to have to make another painful visit.

What Paul displays here is an important description of what the character of our warfare ought to be. We ought not to be looking for a fight. We ought not be quick to fight. Paul's warfare was first and foremost compassionate. And likewise, our first instinct ought to be peace. Paul said in Romans 12:18, "If possible, so far as it depends on you, live peaceably with all." He said to the Galatian church, "So then, as we have opportunity, let us do good to everyone, and especially to those who are of the household of faith" (Gal 6.10).

We are in a war, but our first goal should be peace. It's unfortunately a very strong temptation, especially for young men who are committed to truth, to go looking for a fight. We're tempted to jump into battle mode the second we see something we disagree with, or some sort of theological error. The impulse to defend truth is good and necessary, but like Paul, our first strategy should be the meekness and gentleness of Christ; humility; entreating those who need to hear our message.

But, like Paul, we must be willing to stand and fight if we have to. He says, "I will show boldness if I have to." Our warfare ought to be compassionate, but it must also be courageous. Compassionate courage. Courageous compassion. That ought to characterize our warfare as Christians living in this present age.

THE WEAPONS OF OUR WARFARE

So the authority for our warfare is God's Word, and the character of our warfare ought to be compassionate courage. But then Paul moves on to a description of our warfare itself. Paul is both answering the accusations of the false apostles *and* describing the nature of his conflict with them—how he plans to confront them if they do not respond well to his gentle entreaty. If we have to fight, here's the nature of our warfare as citizens of the redemptive kingdom.

First, he addresses their accusation—they "suspect Paul of walking according to the flesh" (v2). As he alludes to throughout the letter, the false apostles were accusing him of fleshly motives and fleshly methods in his ministry, and so he addresses this accusation of fleshly warfare head on here.

Now, he acknowledges first that we do indeed walk in the flesh: "For though we walk in the flesh," he says in verse 3. The word "flesh" here is just a neutral word that refers to physical, earthly existence. Paul is just saying, "I am human." I am "fleshly" in that sense. In other words, we are in the world; we are fleshly beings. As we have seen throughout this book, there are good earthly necessities that we engage in simply because we walk in the flesh as citizens of God's common kingdom. We eat and drink. We work. We engage in commerce, and physical exercise, and human vocation, and politics, and other God-ordained earthly activities. They are good and necessary as fleshly beings who live on earth.

But though we walk in the flesh, we are not waging war according to the flesh. We do not war according to the flesh, because our war is not a fleshly war. The very nature of our war is not fleshly; it is a spiritual war. That is where the battle really is.

Of course, it's very easy to be tempted to think otherwise because the enemies and warfare most immediately apparent to us is what we can *see* around us. For Paul, his opponents in this case were men of flesh. For us today, false teachers are men and women of flesh. Even more broadly, all of the attacks against Christianity that we see in our day are committed by men and women of flesh.

We can see and identify our enemies, can we not? We can name them. They are false teachers like Creflo Dollar and Joyce Meyer. They are advocates of "woke" Christianity like Eric Mason and Thabiti Anyabwile. They are atheist apologists like Richard Dawkins and Christopher Hitchens. They are identifiable groups like Planned Parenthood or Black Lives Matter or LGTBQ+ activists. They are people in our society who want to murder babies and trans our kids. We can see them; we can identify them; we can name them. These are enemies in the flesh.

SPIRITUAL ENEMIES

But ultimately, our battle is not a battle of flesh. As Paul says in Ephesians 6:12,

> For we do not wrestle against flesh and blood, but against the rulers, against the authorities, against the cosmic powers over this present darkness, against the spiritual forces of evil in the heavenly places.

The true enemies are not of flesh, and therefore we ought not wage war according to the flesh.

We are in the world, but not of the world. We participate in the normal, good, common grace aspects of this earth, but when it comes to the spiritual war in which we are engaged, we do not use fleshly weapons. As Paul says in verse 4,

> For the weapons of our warfare are not of the flesh . . . (2 Cor 10:4)

But unfortunately, as people who do walk in the flesh, we are often tempted to war according to the flesh. As we wage spiritual warfare, we are tempted to use fleshly weapons.

Well-meaning Christians, even pastors, attempting to battle truly evil people and ideologies often fall into the trap of using fleshly methodology to do so. We use human ingenuity or clever fleshly methodology. Some use self assertion, shrewd marketing, business strategies, human reason, entertainment, technology, all in a fleshly attempt to win spiritual battles. Or, we see devilish problems in society around us, and we attempt to use worldly ideologies to battle spiritual problems, or we think that political might will destroy our enemies. Even our measure of success in our warfare begins to become fleshly—we judge success by numbers, by prestige, by cultural acceptance, by political influence.

All of these fleshly weapons may appear to be affective, but in reality they are weak; they may have external success, but they are not actually addressing the true spiritual enemies. We can use fleshly methods and get external conformity, but that's all we get. This was the problem with medieval Christendom, where men like Holy Roman Emperor Charlemagne forced pagans to be baptized. This accomplished fleshly victory, but not spiritual victory. Fleshly weapons yield only fleshly victories.

We can build huge mega-churches with business strategies and marketing techniques, but fleshly weapons achieve only fleshly results. We can fight against evil ideologies with fleshly philosophy or fleshly political might, and we might score some points; we might achieve external fleshly results. But that's all we'll get with fleshly weapons. We're not *really* achieving any victories.

Fleshly weapons like these may appear powerful, but they are nothing compared to spiritual weapons. Notice again verse 4:

> For the weapons of our warfare are not of the flesh but have divine power to destroy strongholds. (2 Cor 10:4)

Fleshly weapons have immediate fleshly success, but spiritual weapons have divine power! Spiritual weapons have divine power to destroy strongholds—they can demolish apparently impregnable fortresses against which no fleshly weapon would have a chance. This term "strongholds" is obviously a metaphor, but a metaphor of what? He tells us in the next verse:

> We destroy arguments and every lofty opinion raised against the knowledge of God ... (2 Cor 10:5)

The strongholds that divine weapons have power to destroy are arguments and lofty opinions raised against the knowledge of God. This is why our weapons must be spiritual, because the true enemies we fight are not flesh and blood but spiritual—arguments and opinions, what Paul calls in 1 Corinthians 3:19, "the wisdom of this world." Defeating fleshly enemies requires fleshly weapons, but defeating spiritual enemies requires spiritual weapons.

These enemies against which we fight are in the realm of ideas—arguments and lofty opinions. Our enemies are not really Creflo Dollar and Joyce Meyer but prosperity gospel arguments. Not really Eric Mason and Thabiti Anyabwile, but woke ideology. Not really Richard Dawkins and Christopher Hitchens, but lofty atheistic opinions. Not really people who want to kill babies and trans kids, our enemies are really arguments and lofty opinions raised against the knowledge of God.

The enemies in our warfare are not really flesh and blood, but ideas. It is these *ideas* raised against the knowledge of God that dominate our society. When you look around you, and you see secularism and rampant atheism, the murder of babies and transing of kids, we need to learn to recognize that the ultimate enemies there are not actually the external atrocities, though they are horrible; the ultimate enemies are arguments and every lofty opinion raised against the knowledge of God.

And so we need divine weapons. Because with divine weapons we actually destroy those ideological strongholds—we destroy the real enemies, the spiritual ideas raised against the knowledge of God.

Now don't misunderstand me. Fleshly weapons are sometimes necessary to fight fleshly battles because as we have seen, we are citizens of God's common kingdom. The Bible does not teach pacifism. If someone threatens the flesh of those in your family or under your care, you take fleshly weapons and defend them. God has indeed appointed government to use fleshly weapons to protect its citizens from fleshly harm. Remember, we do walk in the flesh. Sometimes we have to fight fleshly battles and take fleshly captives. But we must not mistake that for our spiritual warfare and divine spiritual weapons.

With divine weapons we can, as Paul continues in verse 5, "take every *thought* captive to obey Christ." Notice the enemies we are taking captive: not fleshly captives, ideological captives—*thought* captives. Through the use of spiritual, divine weapons, we take captives for Christ—we assert Christ's Lordship over them, but not over fleshly *people*, not over false teachers and authors, not over activists and politicians, not over magistrates and nations; we assert Christ's Lordship over arguments and opinions and thoughts. We wield spiritual weapons of Christ's lordship over spiritual enemies.

SPIRITUAL WEAPONS

So what then are these spiritual, divine weapons that destroy arguments and lofty opinions and take captive thoughts?

It's important here to emphasize that even though we may recognize that our enemies are truly in the realm of ideas, still we must not be tempted to battle thoughts with worldly weapons. We cannot battle false human philosophies with other human philosophies. Remember the way Paul opens this section: he emphasizes his apostolic authority. He is emphasizing that the spiritual weapons we employ in this spiritual warfare must be derived from the authoritative Word of God.

So many are tempted to question whether the Bible is *really* sufficient to give us the weapons to destroy false ideas. Is the Bible *really* enough to fight against unbelief? Surely we need human reason and sophisticated philosophical arguments and scientific evidence to prove the existence of God to skeptics in ways that the Bible can't, because they don't believe the Bible. Is the Bible *really* enough to fight against prejudice and injustice? Maybe we need analytical tools like critical theory, which has been designed to combat injustice in ways that the Bible isn't really equipped to do.

But remember where Paul began: the foundational authority for our warfare is the Word of God, and the Word of God is sufficient as the source of our weapons of warfare. And indeed, the sufficient Word gives us our weapons. In Ephesians 6, after Paul tells us that we do not wage war against flesh and blood, he tells us what our weapons are:

> Therefore take up the whole armor of God, that you may be able to withstand in the evil day, and having done all, to stand firm. [14] Stand therefore, having fastened on the belt of truth, and having put on the breastplate of righteousness, [15] and, as shoes for your feet, having put on the readiness given by the gospel of peace. [16] In all circumstances take up the shield of faith, with which you can extinguish all the flaming darts of the evil one; [17] and take the helmet of salvation, and the sword of the Spirit, which is the word of God, [18] praying at all times in the Spirit, with all

prayer and supplication. To that end, keep alert with all perseverance, making supplication for all the saints. (Eph 6:13-18)

You see, we have already been equipped with the divine spiritual weapons we need. Spiritual virtues like faith and righteousness and truth and our very salvation itself is our armor. And not only must we receive our weapons from the Word of God, the Bible itself is a living and active sword. Our divine, spiritual weapons are what we refer to as the ordinary means of grace. The Word of God pierces to the division of soul and of spirit, of joints and of marrow, and discerns the thoughts and intentions of the heart (Heb 4:12). The Word of God is exactly the weapon we need to battle *thoughts* and take them captive for Christ.

Consider how Paul combated unbelief in his ministry.

And Paul went in, as was his custom, and on three Sabbath days he reasoned with them from the Scriptures. (Acts 17:2)

This is exactly what Paul is defending. He is saying, "I did not come to you with fleshly weapons; I did not come with worldly wisdom; I did not come with clever methods; I did not come with physical force. I reasoned from the Scriptures." Consider how he described his ministry in 2 Corinthians 6:

We put no obstacle in anyone's way, so that no fault may be found with our ministry, [4] but as servants of God we commend ourselves in every way: by great endurance, in afflictions, hardships, calamities, [5] beatings, imprisonments, riots, labors, sleepless nights, hunger; [6] by purity, knowledge, patience, kindness, the Holy Spirit, genuine love; [7] by truthful speech, and the power of God; with the weapons of righteousness for the right hand and for the left; [8] through honor and dishonor, through slander and praise. We are treated as impostors, and yet are true; [9] as unknown, and yet well known; as dying, and behold, we live; as punished, and yet not killed; [10] as sorrowful, yet always rejoicing; as poor, yet making many rich; as having nothing, yet possessing everything. (2 Cor 6:3-10)

These are the weapons we must use in the battle, because what we're after is not simply external victory. We could "win" battles with fleshly weapons; we could score points, we could gain external victory, we could take people physically captive with fleshly weapons, or we could force them into conformity at the point of a sword, but that is not our goal. Our goal is to take every thought captive to the obedience of Christ. Submission to Christ is what we're after. Obedience to Christ. Voluntary submission. What we're after is the salvation of souls and sanctification of Christians. We're not just aiming for external conformity; we're looking for internal obedience.

We must use spiritual weapons, because it is a spiritual mission we have been given by Christ: make disciples. We do this through gospel preaching, through baptizing new believers and joining them to local churches where their thoughts are then progressively taken captive to obey Christ as they are discipled with the ordinary means of grace, these spiritual weapons that have divine power to destroy strongholds.

So these spiritual weapons of the Word destroy unbelief leading to salvation, and then these same spiritual weapons are what continue to progressively take every thought captive to obey Christ—this is Christian sanctification.

This is why it is essential that a focus be kept upon clear, sustained exposition of God's *thinking*. If we recognize that our enemy is *really* unbiblical *thinking*, then our *primary* weapon will be careful, sustained preaching and explanation of God's *thinking*. Many Christians are ignorant of the most basic doctrines of the Christian faith. No wonder they are easy prey to devilish thinking.

> But though this world, with devils filled,
> should threaten to undo us,
> we will not fear, for God has willed
> his truth to triumph through us.
> The prince of darkness grim,
> we tremble not for him;

> his rage we can endure,
> for lo! his doom is sure;
> one little word shall fell him.[1]

If you're concerned by the way godless ideologies are plaguing our society, then go to church—that is where the weapons are. Our *primary* battlefield is not in the political sphere or among the elite culture-makers, our primary battlefield is what we do when we gather as the church—the ordinary means of grace. Preaching, prayer, singing, Scripture reading, baptism, the Lord's Table—these are the weapons of our warfare. This is our battlefield.

Worship is warfare.

If you want to battle the real enemies, don't use fleshly weapons; don't trust in philosophy, don't trust in politics, don't trust in clever marketing techniques, trust in the divine, spiritual weapons of the Word.

> That Word above all earthly powers
> no thanks to them abideth;
> the Spirit and the gifts are ours
> through him who with us sideth.
> Let goods and kindred go,
> this mortal life also;
> the body they may kill:

---

[1] Martin Luther, "A Mighty Fortress Is Our God" (1529), trans. Frederick Hedge (1852).

God's truth abideth still;
his kingdom is forever!

GO INTO THE SANCTUARY OF GOD

When we observe bad things around us like the moral decay we're seeing today, we are often tempted to take up fleshly weapons. *We need more laws! Stronger government! More political engagement by Christians!* We're tempted to despair. We're tempted to give up. This is what Asaph experienced in Psalm 73, when he said, "But as for me, my feet had almost stumbled, my steps had nearly slipped. For I was envious of the arrogant when I saw the prosperity of the wicked."

But the biblical answer is not fleshly weapons. As Paul says in 2 Corinthians 5, we walk by faith and not by sight. As Paul says a chapter earlier in 2 Corinthians 4:8-9,

> We are afflicted in every way, but not crushed; perplexed, but not driven to despair; [9] persecuted, but not forsaken; struck down, but not destroyed.

How can we have the same response as Paul to the wickedness around us and the pain and suffering we experience? He says a few verses later in 2 Corinthians 4:16-18,

> So we do not lose heart. Though our outer self is wasting away, our inner self is being renewed day by day.

> [17] For this light momentary affliction is preparing for us an eternal weight of glory beyond all comparison, [18] as we look not to the things that are seen but to the things that are unseen. For the things that are seen are transient, but the things that are unseen are eternal.

We recognize that there is more than meets the eye, and seeing with the eyes of faith helps us to endure under the pressures of this world and resist the temptations of the wicked. This light momentary affliction is not the reality—the reality is unseen and eternal, an eternal weight of glory beyond all comparison.

And this is exactly what solved Asaph's problem in Psalm 73. After describing the apparent prosperity of the wicked, he says in Psalm 73:16–17,

> But when I thought how to understand this, it seemed to me a wearisome task, [17] until I went into the sanctuary of God; then I discerned their end.

In the sanctuary of God, Asaph is enabled to see the unseen, eternal reality with eyes of faith.

You see, the solution for when we are tempted to despair or take up fleshly weapons because of wickedness and pain and suffering in our lives is to go to the sanctuary of God, to the public worship of God's people in God's presence.

Corporate worship is where we come to renew our inner selves. We come to the sanctuary of God so that we are more and more able to see the things that are unseen and not look to the things that are seen. For the things that are seen are transient, but the things that are unseen are eternal.

We are currently sojourners in a wilderness, and we have a portable tabernacle into which we can enter through the atoning sacrifice of Christ. And as we gather as the sanctuary of God on the Lord's Day, we experience a foretaste of the highest heaven, the true temple, which will come in its fullness at the return of the King. In that Day, the heavenly sanctuary will come down to earth. In that day, the whole earth will be the sanctuary of God, "to unite all things in him, things in heaven and things on earth" (Eph 1:10). This was God's plan from the beginning.

> And I heard a loud voice from the throne saying, "Behold, the dwelling place of God is with man. He will dwell with them, and they will be his people, and God himself will be with them as their God. [4] He will wipe away every tear from their eyes, and death shall be no more, neither shall there be mourning, nor crying, nor pain anymore, for the former things have passed away." (Rev 21:3-4)

Until then, let us be faithful to go to the sanctuary and worship God as he has instructed us, where we have the joy to join our feeble earthly worship with the real worship of the highest heaven, joining our voices and hearts with the angels who forever surround the throne and with the saints who have gone before us. This is a foretaste of that final day when a great multitude that no one can number will be in the presence of Jesus worshiping him.

CONCLUSION

What I have attempted to provide in this book is a brief sketch of a conservative Christian posture toward culture more faithful to Scripture than much of what constitutes the prevailing evangelical perspectives. Despite caricatures by opponents, and extreme abuses by some, this philosophy provides a basis for a rather robust philosophy of cultural engagement.

Why is it so important to have our motivation right about how we live in society? Why is it important that we don't try to motivate ourselves and others with grand ambitions of societal transformation?

First, God never promised grand societal transformation, and so if we make that our goal, it can lead to deep discouragement. I know some people who are very active in trying to push for massive social change, and they're some of the grumpiest and at times angriest people I know. Why? Because they're not seeing results. They're discouraged. They may see little advances here or there, but certainly not the kind of massive social change they *think* God has promised them. And often times, those kinds of people end up burning out. How many big-name Christians have we seen burn out and fall away from the faith in just the past several years? God never commands us to do massive, amazing, earth shattering things in society. He commands us to be holy and faithful.

Second, when societal transformation is our goal, we inevitably lose our mission as the church. If our central mission as a church becomes anything other than making disciples—and even as individuals, if our central mission is grand societal transformation, history has shown that we end up losing the gospel. But if our goal as churches is making disciples who are holy and faithful in society, and if our goal as individual Christians is holiness and faithfulness in society, then we just may have at least a small influence.

Third, when societal transformation is our goal, we fail to recognize the value of the "ordinary"—common vocations and ordinary people. We tend to buy into a celebretyism that praises the larger-than-life people and undervalues faithful, ordinary people. We want heroes, when we should deeply value regular, faithful fathers and mothers and grandparents and pastors and fellow brothers and sisters in Christ. We chase after big movements and causes, failing to recognize the value of normal, everyday faithfulness of rearing godly children, working hard in our vocations, performing our civic duty in the political sphere, and simply doing it all for God's glory. And even in the church, we tend to chase after spectacle, big programs, and large causes, rather than trusting the week-by-week ordinary means of grace that disciple us into holy, faithful Christians.

Fourth, actually having significant influence in society almost always requires compromise. This is the main point of James Davison Hunter's book, *To Change the World*. He shows that in order to really change the world on a massive scale, we would need to get in positions of power, and in order to get into positions of power, we have to give into the idea that earthly power is where real change takes place, essentially compromising our trust in the sufficiency of God's Word and the fact that real transformation happens in the human soul through the gospel.

But we see this happening don't we? People who want to change the world try to work their way into positions of power, and you can't do that by boldly proclaiming the gospel and standing for holiness. Instead, you have to get those currently in power to accept you, which means you water down your message. And this is what's behind when you hear elite evangelicals piously proclaim "the world is watching" as a defense for privatized religion. *Don't be bold in your stand against the murder of the preborn—the world is watching; they'll think we're being mean to women. No, we need to be more nuanced in our approach so that the world will accept us, and then we can get into those places of influence.* This is why you really don't see very many truly faithful, set apart Christians who are committed to their local church and holy living getting into high political roles. How many truly faithful Christians have become Senators? Some. Not many. How many truly faithful Christians have become the President of the

United States? It is very, very difficult—not impossible, but difficult—to get into positions of power and influence and still remain faithful to what God has called us to be as Christians.

I love how James Davison Hunter summarizes the kind of Christian faithfulness I have advocated as Christians living in society—our lives ought to be characterized by faithful presence. Another way to think of it is that we are to live lives of submission to others and their needs. It is instructive that when Peter describes how we ought to live in various kinds of everyday relationships, submission is part of our responsibility.

> 1 Peter 2:13—"Be subject to every human institution."

> 1 Peter 2:18—"Be subject to your masters."

> 1 Peter 3:1—"Wives, be subject to your husbands."

> 1 Peter 3:7—"Likewise, husbands live with your wives in an understanding way, showing them honor."

Our lives in society ought not to be characterized by trying to get ahead, trying to advance our own agenda, or trying to do what's best for us; our goal in society ought to be to submit ourselves to the needs of others—submit to governing authority, submit to our employer, submit to the needs of others in our families.

Our goal in society is not grand scale societal change or cultural transformation—we cannot be Second Adams. We ought simply to live holy lives, demonstrate kindness toward all people, and apply what it means to be a Christian in whatever cultural sphere God has called us. And as a church—as a redemptive kingdom community—we ought to make disciples, gathering more redemptive kingdom citizens and teaching them how to obey Christ in their everyday lives.

This philosophy, I believe, is more faithful to Scripture than the dominant evangelical views today. This biblical understanding protects the unique mission of the church to make disciples and avoids triumphalistic "kingdom" motivation so characteristic of evangelical discussions of Christianity and culture. Setting as our goal the transformation of society almost always results in failure to fulfill the mission Christ gave to his church. Most examples of evangelical desire to "transform culture" are little more than trying to be accepted by the culture. As Andy Crouch has astutely observed, "The rise of interest in cultural transformation has been accompanied by a rise in cultural transformation of a different sort—the transformation of the church into the culture's image."[1]

In other words, a biblical philosophy of culture does not understand our role in society to be in terms of

---

[1] Andy Crouch, *Culture Making: Recovering Our Creative Calling* (Downers Grove: InterVarsity Press, 2008), 189.

cultural redemption or "work for the kingdom." Rather, we should view the church's exclusive mission as one of evangelization and discipling Christians to live sanctified lives in whatever cultural sphere God has called us. This is the extent of our "responsibility" toward culture, and anything more than this threatens to sideline what Christ has actually commanded us to do.

There's a sort of frantic restlessness that inherently characterizes the goal of massive societal transformation; but there is a restful contentment that accompanies a life of Christian faithfulness that says, "I am going to submit to the authority of God's Word; I am going to rest in the ordinary means of grace; and I am going to work hard at rearing godly children, working heartily as unto the Lord, standing up for righteousness in society, and doing it all for God's glory."

We live faithfully in this present age, fully optimistic that the Second Adam will accomplish God's plan for human history "when he comes on that day to be glorified in his saints, and to be marveled at among all who have believed" (2 Thess 1:10).

APPENDIX

REVIEW OF *MERE CHRISTENDOM* BY DOUGLAS WILSON

When Stephen Wolfe's book *The Case for Christian Nationalism* first came out, I picked up a copy, read the first third of the book, and then decided that it wasn't really relevant to me at the time. I had written and taught about the biblical relationship between Christianity and culture for over a decade, had fairly firm convictions on the matter, and recognized quickly that I disagreed theologically with Wolfe's proposal. It was immediately evident to me that his proposal was essentially an application of paedobaptism and postmillennialism to whole nations and, well, as a non-postmillennial Baptist, I didn't think it was relevant.[1]

However, earlier this year I began to see a number of young men start praising Wolfe's book, using

---

[1] Stephen Wolfe is not postmillennial, but my sense when I read his book and started hearing about Christian Nationalism was that it was an application of paedobaptism to nations as a natural expression of postmillennial eschatology, which Wilson's book bears out.

phraseology like "baptize the nations," asserting that the purpose of government is to orient individuals toward Christianity, aggressively calling for the application of Mosaic law to the nation, and loudly proclaiming that Christian Nationalism is the only way to beat back the onslaught of pagan secularism. And many of these young men were Baptist and not postmillennial.

So I read the rest of Wolfe's book as well as Andrew Torba and Andrew Isker's *Christian Nationalism: A Biblical Guide to Taking Dominion and Discipling Nations*, and then I began to make statements online about how what these men were proposing was inherently incompatible with Baptist theology and essentially amounted to postmillennial theonomy. I became concerned about the latent white supremacy appearing at the fringes of the movement and the growing language of agitation that accompanied much of the (quite understandable) angst regarding the quickly devolving condition of our country.

So when Canon Press sent me Doug Wilson's forthcoming book that articulates his vision for *Mere Christendom*, something he has discussed over the years on his blog, my interest was piqued. I wondered how the proposal from this elder statesman of postmillennial theonomy would compare to the recent Christian nationalist language I had read in print and was seeing online.

Wilson's book did not disappoint.

Not that I agree with his vision. As a Baptist who is not postmillennial, I do not. But that's exactly the point.

Wilson's *Mere Christendom* confirms two important ideas I have been trying to make in the current debates: (1) building Christian nations is inherently a postmillennial/paedobaptist project, and (2) forming a robust Christian public theology does not require Christian Nationalism.

The book has four parts, the first two presenting the vision for Christendom and the latter two discussing the practical details. In the first section, Wilson characterizes the current mess we are in, and in the second he sets forth his proposal for what he calls "mere Christendom." In the third part, Wilson describes what such a Christendom would look like, particularly dealing with issues related to free speech, and in the fourth part he articulates what he believes would be necessary to build it. Wilson believes we *must* pursue mere Christendom since "secularism has run its course and does not have the wherewithal to resist the demands of radical Islam. Or a radical anything else, for that matter" (69).

WILSON'S VISION FOR A MERE CHRISTENDOM

Wilson defines Mere Christendom as "a network of nations bound together by a formal, public, civic acknowledgment of the Lordship of Jesus Christ, and the fundamental truth of the Apostles' Creed" (69). This does not mean a tax-funded established church, but an established church nonetheless, "in the sense that the magistrate has the responsibility to recognize her, to convene synods and councils to seek her counsel, and to listen to her" (70).

His vision for a mere Christendom is predicated upon three fundamental theological presuppositions, the first of which I affirm with qualification, and the latter two with which I disagree.

THE MYTH OF NEUTRALITY

The first foundation is the myth of neutrality. He asserts, "The public square cannot be neutral" (4). He wants to wake up Christians to the reality that "One of the central tactics of our regnant secularism is to pretend that their foundational assumptions are religiously neutral, and that we need not look at them" (35). He quotes Christian Reconstructionist R. J. Rushdoony's famous maxim, "not whether but which" (143). Wilson is convinced that accepting the myth of neutrality has led many Christians to stand idly by while Christendom crumbles in the face of secular liberalism. Instead, Christians ought to recognize that secularism is actually an alternative religion that seeks to cast off the Lordship of Christ.

On this point I agree with Wilson. There is no neutrality on any issue; every matter is either consistent with God's law or it contradicts God's law. There is only right or wrong, good or bad, light or dark. And secularism is a false religion.

Where I disagree with Wilson is in the implications he draws from this principle. Wilson argues that since there is no neutrality in politics, then the only two alternatives are anarchy (secular theocracy) or theonomy (Christian theocracy). "The Lordship of Christ is not an option that we might select from a row of numerous options," Wilson argues. "It is Christ or chaos. It is Christ or Antichrist" (70). He believes that the founding of this nation was possible only because it was explicitly Christian: "Republics do not exist without republican virtue. And virtue does not exist apart from the grace of God, as offered in the message of the death and resurrection of Jesus Christ" (114).

The problem is that Wilson does not seem to give any space for common grace, the *imago Dei*, and the reality of "when Gentiles, who do not have the law, by nature do what the law requires ... even though they do not have the law. They show that the work of the law is written on their hearts, while their conscience also bears witness, and their conflicting thoughts accuse or even excuse them" (Rom 2:14–15). This is what Greg Bahnsen referred to as "borrowed capital"—pagans borrowing biblical values in certain areas of their lives. Even though it is inconsistent with what they say they believe, pagans made in God's image nevertheless sometimes take advantage of his common grace and do what the law requires.

I do believe that the only grounding for successful

living that makes consistent sense is one rooted in the authoritative truth of God's holy Word and repentant faith in Jesus Christ. When it comes to eternal salvation, it's Christ or chaos. Yet because all men are made in the image of God (Gen 1:27), because "the heavens are telling the glory of God" (Ps 19:1) and God's "invisible attributes, namely, his eternal power and divine nature, have been clearly perceived, ever since the creation of the world, in the things that have been made" (Rom 1:20), and because God shows common grace even to the unjust (Matt 5:45), unbelieving people often reflect a transcendent morality in their lives that in actuality is inconsistent with their belief system.

"There can be no true liberty that is not grounded in transcendentals" (147). Agreed. "Secularism has no transcendent ground for anything" (138). That's true for secularism. But even pagans throughout history have sought to build their political systems on transcendental realities, even though they could not fully account for those realities. I would quickly agree with Wilson that such philosophical grounding is inconsistent with pagan belief and makes most sense from within a biblical worldview, but nevertheless, what Quentin Faulkner has called pagan "world consciousness" is a far cry from Enlightenment secular nominalism. Pagan Greco/Roman thought embodied transcendental grounding for its political philosophy. Wilson believes that "Post-Christian secularists were using Christian capital" (146), and I agree, but other pagans throughout history have done similarly as they apply God's law written on their hearts.

C. S. Lewis makes this observation in both *Mere Christianity* and *The Abolition of Man*, and in the latter he provides an appendix of many examples of civic laws from various nations around the world that are an embodiment of transcendent morality that ultimately comes from God. These are the very laws that we ought to be promoting and supporting in our own legal system. Pagans can recognize the wisdom of these laws and keep them, though in truth to do so is inconsistent with their own pagan worldview. In fact, as Lewis argues, the propensity of even pagans to recognize the wisdom of God's moral law opens wonderful opportunities to preach the written Word to those pagans, offering them true freedom and righteousness in Christ.

Interestingly, Wilson appears to acknowledge this reality. For example, he asserts as axiomatic that "it is *self-evident* that we were endowed by the Creator with certain rights that are inalienable, and that among these rights are the right to life, liberty, and property" (34). He suggests that God has "dropped the yeast of His Word, which included that system of case law into the Greco-Roman loaf" (178), an acknowledgment that even pagan Greco-Roman political philosophy reflected something consistent with a biblical-informed political theology. He references Chesterton's portrayal of "decent (but still lost) pagans of Rome" (209). Wilson chides those in our nation who "try to pretend that they are the only ones in the world who have had these blessings" (203). "Read the story patterns of history," he admonishes—"the rise and fall of empires and great nations is one of the oldest stories in the world" (203). Later in the book, Wilson affirms "informed reason, common grace, natural revelation" (223).

Throughout history, pagans have often figured out successful legal systems that reflect biblical values because, since God designed the world to work in a certain way, those kinds of systems just work, and "stupidity doesn't work" (242). That's the reality of common grace politics.

The truth is that in matters of the state, the only two options are not Christ or chaos. In his kind providence, God specifically designed human government to provide a third common grace option given to all humankind (not just his redeemed people) that imperfectly preserves a degree of order and peace until Christ establishes his perfect theocratic Kingdom on earth. God's covenant with Noah in Genesis 9 reveals God's plan to preserve humankind and creation until the Second Adam establishes his earthly rule. Because of the reality of human rebellion, God provided measures by which in his providence he would preserve the stability of a cursed world through the earthly institution of human government, with its God-given responsibility of capital punishment. Before the Flood, it was Christ or chaos, and it quickly devolved into chaos. After Genesis 9, and especially after Babel, nations formed and prevented chaos as God works his plan of redemption for his people.

I'm afraid many Christians (understandably) want utopia now and they think that can be accomplished by simply asserting Christ's rule over the nations. But imperfect, common grace order is why God created human government, not utopia. Utopia will come when the King comes. But that leads to the next point.

PAEDOCOMMUNION AND POSTMILLENNIALISM

The second and third presuppositions of Wilson's vision are connected: paedocommunion and postmillennialism. He articulates, "The thing these two doctrines share in common is that they are both, in different ways, an optimistic testimony about the course of future generations" (97). He further explains, "Paedocommunion nurtures the next generation in optimistic faith, and postmillennialism is the grounded hope that God will continue to nurture His Church across multiple generations" (97).

It is important to recognize just how critically fundamental these two presuppositions are to Wilson's project. He does not really defend the idea of mere Christendom from a sustained biblical argument; in fact, he quotes very little Scripture at all in this section. This is not necessarily a criticism since he acknowledges his own theological presuppositions; he assumes the biblical validity of paedocommunion and postmillennialism (which he has explained and defended elsewhere), and on the basis of these theological commitments, Wilson builds his vision for mere Christendom.

Wilson's vision is built on the bedrock of these theological presuppositions in two ways. First, Wilson expects Christian parents to baptize their infants, rearing them in the discipline and instruction of the Lord, and that "as children grow up in a faithful covenant home, they *will come* to a genuine profession of faith as a matter of course" (*Standing on the Promises*, 85). That presupposition is essential for Wilson's proposal since it assumes a necessary continued expansion of God's people through their children, which will eventually reach a tipping point that results in a majority of the world's population publicly acknowledging Christ's Lordship.

Further, this theology is necessary for the idea of Christendom implicitly in that to achieve mere Christendom, you essentially "baptize" the nation first (public acknowledgment of Christ's Lordship), and then you press for conversions (internal conviction of Christ's Lordship). I am thankful that throughout the book, Wilson stresses that "formal recognition of the Lordship of Jesus is necessary but not sufficient. More is required than paper commitments" (73). He strongly insists upon "the absolute need for regeneration and the cross of Jesus Christ. It is only a work of the Spirit that can give us new hearts. Christian civilization is absolutely necessary, but without those new hearts, Christian standards of civilization are intolerable, as can be easily verified" (226-27). Nevertheless, as with literal paedocommunion, the assumption is that public, formal acknowledgment of Christ's Lordship by those who have not yet personally professed submission to his Lordship is one means God uses to lead individuals to personal acknowledgment.

Of course, as a Baptist, I don't agree with this fundamental theological foundation. The purpose of Wilson's book is not to provide a thorough defense of these presuppositions, and so I will not attempt to refute them here. However, I would like to press in a bit on why Baptist theology would necessarily preclude any adoption of the mere Christendom proposal.

A central difference between credobaptist and paedobaptist theologies is that Baptists stress that the New Covenant is "not like" (Jer 31:32) the Old Covenant. In the Old Covenant, the sign of the covenant precedes inner regeneration and personal profession of faith. Thus, the covenant people are comprised of both regenerate and unregenerate people. In the New Covenant, however, inner regeneration and personal profession of faith precede the sign of the covenant. Thus, the covenant people are comprised of only those who profess faith in Christ.

Hopefully it is apparent, then, why as a Baptist I would object to calling people "Christian" who have not personally professed faith. Baptists don't expect people to acknowledge Christ's lordship formally and publicly until *after* they actually believe it. In the New Testament, no one is forced to acknowledge the Lordship of Christ—in fact, quite the opposite. Yet this is exactly what would be necessary for anything like "Christian" nations or Christendom.

In terms of the eschatological basis for Wilson's vision, I actually agree with most of what he believes will happen; our difference is a matter of timing. He argues that there are only three options when it comes to building Christendom: "(1) Jesus doesn't care whether or not nations are explicitly Christian. (2) Jesus is opposed to nations being explicitly Christian. (3) Jesus wants nations to be explicitly Christian" (95).

I agree—Jesus does want a theocracy. And he will get what he wants, when he comes again in glory to judge the living and the dead. And it won't be *mere* Christendom—it will be totalitarian, rule-with-a-rod-of iron theocracy. For now, Jesus is presently redeeming his elect while preserving the world through imperfect governments, but one day he will establish Christendom.

Further, even assuming Wilson's presuppositions, his vision for Christendom raises some critical questions that largely go unanswered. First, Wilson says he wants an established Church, but *which Church*? In Wilson's ideal Christian republic, "the Church must be established, in the sense that the magistrate has the responsibility to recognize her, to convene synods and councils to seek her counsel, and to listen to her" (69). Notice the singular "Church." And again I ask, which Church? Maybe in an episcopal or presbyterian form of church government all local churches would be part of a larger body, but what of the Baptists, Congregationalists, and Bible churches? How would they fit in? Again I say, Baptist theology is incompatible with the notion of Christendom.

The second problem stems from the first. In order to achieve a *mere* Christendom in which a Presbyterian Congress is not flogging Baptists, the doctrinal basis for such a "non-sectarian" Christendom (71) must be reduced to the Apostles' Creed. Would Roman Catholics, then, be welcomed to the table of Christendom and recognized as Christians? I can appreciate the value of Presbyterians and Baptists happily affirming one another as Christian and working together on various parachurch ministries, all while maintaining their denominational distinctives at the church level; but if the Apostles' Creed is our only measure of what constitutes Christianity, then we would have to recognize as Christian those who affirm creedal trinitarianism and Christology but who deny justification by grace alone through faith alone in Christ alone. For that matter, Mormons could technically affirm the Apostles' Creed. I am aware that Wilson's church recognizes Roman Catholic baptisms and welcomes them to the Lord's Table, but this Baptist considers Roman Catholicism a false religion.

Third, I am thankful that Wilson's version of

postmillennialism affirms that the goal of Christendom will be achieved only through "preaching, baptizing, and discipleship, and not by campaigning, legislating, punditblogging, and so on" (95). What he proposes cannot occur "apart from the widespread dissemination of the gospel among the people" (118). And he believes that it won't happen any time soon. Wilson definitely has a long view. He criticizes "Christendom 1.0" as being too immature to achieve the goal. However, he never clarifies as to when we would know we're ready for "Christendom 2.0." "The world will gradually come to recognize [Christ's Lordship]," he says, but he never tells us how many need to recognize it before we're ready to publicly and formally acknowledge it.

The biggest reason I object to Wilson's mere Christendom proposal, however, is that we simply do not find anything like it in the New Testament. I understand the broader biblical/theological argument set forth by postmillennialists, and I do believe in the importance of systematic theology. But if God wanted us to establish nations that explicitly designate themselves as "Christian," you would think we'd find even the slightest hint of it in the New Testament epistles.

But we don't. What we find is an emphasis upon the fact that Christians are citizens of a heavenly kingdom (Phil 3:20), that we are pilgrims in this present world (1 Pet 2:11), but that we should care about this world nonetheless (1 Tim 2:1-2).

WILSON'S CHRISTIAN POLITICAL PHILOSOPHY

The second half of Wilson's book is where things get really interesting, because I would suggest that what he offers by way of the practical details of mere Christendom is not exclusively Christendom, but rather how NT Christians ought to think about common grace politics. He moves on from his postmillennial ideal to practically what kind of government rightly takes into account realities in a sin-cursed world. Not only does this non-postmillennial Baptist find much in this second half with which to agree about how Christians should think about government, but also Wilson's articulation of ideal government ought to restrain the more aggressive Christians who quickly call for outlawing anything they (rightly) think is immoral in culture.

Wilson argues that biblically-informed Christians will favor extremely limited government: "This means embracing the biblical doctrine of the nature of man, which means limited government, separation of powers, checks and balances, and federalism, which in turn means a removal of many of the temptations to bring in the kingdom with a sword" (158). He agrees with Jefferson, who famously quipped, "government is best which governs least" (122). Though he quibbles with part of what C. S. Lewis said on the matter, Wilson quotes Lewis on this point:

The loftier the pretensions of the power, the more meddlesome, inhuman and oppressive it will be. Theocracy is the worst of all possible governments. All political power is at best a necessary evil: but it is least evil when its sanctions are most modest and commonplace, when it claims no more than to be useful or convenient and sets itself strictly limited objectives. Anything transcendental or spiritual, or even anything very strongly ethical, in its pretensions is dangerous, and encourages it to meddle with our private lives. (119)

Wilson considers himself a theonomist, but he argues that "a commitment to biblical law" does not mean "we are to bring all the requirements of the old order straight across" (153). Rather, especially because we recognize the biblical doctrine of human depravity, we insist upon limited government where we restrain authoritarian tendencies. "The first thing that would happen in a biblical law order," Wilson suggests, "is that the EPA, the IRS, the Department of Education, etc. would all be abolished. Legitimate functions of government (Defense, State, etc.) would be significantly downsized or redirected" (72–73). He argues, "What governmental power exists must be fixed, defined, nailed down, watched very carefully, even though it is swathed in the duct tape of multiple Bible verses about man's depravity" (123). Thus, Wilson actually describes himself as a "theocratic libertarian" (120).

Wilson applies this specifically in two chapters to the biblical necessity of free speech and therefore avoiding the restraint of blasphemy by the power of the state. While as a theonomist Wilson believes in "the need to restore the Bible as the quarry from which to obtain the needed stone for our foundations of social order" (149), he strongly argues against state imposed punishment for blasphemy. He reminds us that "those who want the government to have the right to kill blasphemers are also asking for the government to have the right to kill those who rebuke their blasphemies" (157), and "When you give the state power to punish a blasphemer, you are giving the state the power to blaspheme with impunity" (171). Since rulers are sinners, a healthy recognition of the depravity of man ought to restrain us from giving them the kind of power that would be required to punish blasphemy. "Whenever you give the state plenipotentiary powers to crack down on x, y, and z, what you are actually doing—please remember this—is giving them plenipotentiary powers to commit x, y, and z" (173).

Therefore, "It is better to allow a troubled individual to blaspheme than to give, for the sake of preventing such things, regulatory powers over the definition of blasphemy to the very people most likely to be tempted to get into real blasphemy" (175-76). Wilson calls this "restraining the worst blasphemer first" (the title of Chapter 11).

It's not that we Christians don't want to eradicate blasphemy—we do. But "we are not waging war according to the flesh" (2 Cor 10:3); "the artillery of the new covenant is more powerful than what the people of God had in their possession in the old covenant" (169). We want to eliminate blasphemy, but "not through the law" (158); rather, we do so through gospel conversion. "The central way that Christians are called to transform the world is not to be found in politics," Wilson insists (221). "Christ gave us our mission and He gave us our methods. The world is to be brought to Christ, with all the nations submitting to Him, agreeing to obey Him. That is the mission. The method consisted of Word and water, bread and wine" (160). Amen.

Wilson argues that inherent protection of free speech by limiting the state's power "is the theopolitical genius of Christianity" (171). He argues that "The founding of our nation really was exceptional, because the men who drafted our Constitution knew that American politicians, taking one thing with another, would be every bit as sleazy as the same class of men from any other clime" (201). I agree.

However, I would suggest that the U. S. Founders, many of whom professed Christ or at least operated from within the heritage of Christendom, penned the Constitution not with the intent to establish a Christian nation, but rather with the intent to *break* from the notion of Christendom because they recognized the inherent problems with established religion. Wilson himself quotes John Adams's infamous assertion that the U. S. republic was founded on "reason, morality, and the Christian religion," while very quickly admitting that Adams was himself Unitarian, "the granddaddy of all the errors of American civic religion" (71). The very founder Wilson quotes to prove that the United States was established as a Christian nation would not fit into a mere Christendom that had the Apostles' Creed as its basis. Adams was not a Christian. Instead, he was a pagan who was articulating something more like Romans 2 common grace morality cloaked in biblical language. In other words, protection of free speech by limiting the state's power is actually the theopolitical genius of those who recognized the abuse of power perpetrated by nations with established religion (i.e., Christendom).

Historically, Western Christendom did not favor limited government but the imposition of Christianity through the establishment of religion. The governments of historic Christendom were quite totalitarian, imprisoning, punishing, and even killing those who dared dissent. The founding of America was not an expression of Christendom, it was a repudiation of establishment religion inherent to Christendom. On the other hand, I also may acknowledge that America would likely not have been possible without Christendom. Perhaps a parallel might be that Reformation theology would not have developed with the depth that it did without the heretical teachings of Rome, but that doesn't mean that we give Rome credit for Reformation theology. Similarly,

America's federal democratic republic probably would not have developed as exceptionally as it did without the blessings and abuses of Christendom, but that doesn't mean we long for Christendom once again.

So I agree with Wilson that faithful Christians who have anything to say about government should actively limit its power (159). He rightly observes, "Requiring government to remain modest and within the bounds of sanity is therefore one of the most profound ethical requirements that has ever been promulgated among men" (122). But this is not uniquely theonomic—it's simply the best way for government to operate in a sin-cursed world.

CHRISTIAN FAITHFULNESS

At the end of the day, then, though I disagree with Wilson's mere Christendom proposal, rooted as it is in paedocommunionist and postmillennial presuppositions, I believe Wilson's political philosophy accurately captures what Scripture teaches regarding a Christian's interaction with the state. I'm firmly with him that Christians need a "robust theology of resistance" when the state oversteps its jurisdiction and that "we are to be among the best citizens a magistrate ever had—we should be diligent and hard-working, dutiful and responsible, so that we might put to silence the ignorance of foolish men" (213).

Where I may differ practically from Wilson and his

followers is when they trend toward what I would characterize as political agitation. Though I believe we ought to call public leaders to repentance, we ought to resist when the state attempts to impose its will upon the church, we ought to loudly decry the immoral atrocities of our day (abortion, gay "marriage," transgenderism, and child mutilation), and we ought to boldly proclaim the Lordship of Christ in the public square, I'm not sure what real value there is in posting billboards just to poke at pagans or intentionally disobeying the state on matters that don't actually prohibit the church's free worship. I'm not sure how this is "leading a peaceful and quiet life, godly and dignified in every way" (1 Tim 2:2) and obeying the command to "if possible, so far as it depends on you, live peaceably with all" (Rom 12:18).

One of the important things about Wilson's articulation is that it ought to chasten many of those recently quick to jump on the Christian Nationalism bandwagon. He admonishes those "on the right who gladly welcome sobriquets like Christian nationalist, but who then receive it like it was the very latest blasphemous selection from the fruit club, with all the cherries, my only word to them is that they should repent and knock it off. Driving your pick-up around town with that huge Trump flag flapping on one side and the Let's Go Brandon in the original Greek waving on the other . . . isn't helping anything" (85). He chides those who think that the cultural predicament we are in is anything new: "Cultural decadence is something that has happened routinely to civilizations for millennia, and it is a sign of our cultural narcissism that we are somehow surprised by it happening to us. The surprise is not sincere; it is not honestly come by. Somebody really ought to read a book" (223). And he cautions those Christians who ultimately diagnose our problems and propose solutions primarily in political terms: "Our problem is not globalization, for pity's sake. Our problem is unbelief, and it is a very boring and ancient form of unbelief. We are about as unique as a pint of salt water a hundred miles off the coast of Hawaii" (235).

And most of all, I love the kind of Christian faithfulness that Wilson consistently proposes as our primary task in this age: strong Christian marriages, godly Christian parents faithfully bringing up their children in the discipline and instruction of the Lord, fervent gospel proclamation, holy living, and covenant-renewal worship that is regulated by Scripture instead of wracked by worldliness. I fully agree with him that our first task is to clean house: "Christ is the only Savior. Christ really is Lord of Heaven and earth. But our immediate task is not to get the world to confess that. Our first and most pressing task is to get over twenty percent of evangelical and Reformed leadership to confess it. Then we would really be getting somewhere" (230). I especially love this:

> In the face of the kind of evil that is abroad in the world, evangelical Christians need to stop filling up

their worship services with sentimentalist treacle and to start worshiping biblically in a very dark world. We are confronted with a great and growing evil, and we are discovering that we do not have the liturgical vocabulary to respond to it appropriately at all. When we sing or pray the psalms, all of them, there are two consequences that should be mentioned. One, we are praying in the will of God, and He hears such prayers. Second, we discover that praying and singing biblically transforms us. This really is the need of the hour. (227-28)

Amen and amen.

Yet my conviction is that all of Wilson's emphasis on Christian Faithfulness and limited government that protects free speech can be biblically defended and cheerfully pursued without his theological presuppositions or some sort of Christian Nationalism. And that is a key point: I do not see anything in Wilson's proposal about how we ought to build Christendom that a faithful Christian should not already be doing.

If I could be convinced from Scripture of paedocommunion and postmillennialism, I would enthusiastically pursue Mere Christendom. But, alas, convincing me of such would take a Millennium.

www.ingramcontent.com/pod-product-compliance
Lightning Source LLC
Chambersburg PA
CBHW051124160426
43195CB00014B/2332